AN INTRODUCTION TO POLITICS

This is a little book to remove painlessly some of the passion, prejudice and ignorance that cloud political discussion; a book to deepen the general reader's understanding of what politics is really about. Holding the past and the present, and the ideal and the real, in just balance, Professor Laski examines the nature of the state and its organisation, how it meets the needs of those composing it, and how it is being forced more and more inevitably into a wider whole: a world government. Never was it more necessary that these principles, fundamental to human organisation all over the world, should be universally understood.

GW00806338

BY HAROLD J. LASKI

A Grammar of Politics
Liberty in the Modern State
Parliamentary Government in England
The State in Theory and Practice
The Strategy of Freedom
Reflections on the Revolution of our Time
Democracy in Crisis
The Rise of European Liberalism
The American Presidency
The Danger of Being a Gentleman
The Foundations of Sovereignty
Studies in Law and Politics
An Introduction to Politics
Karl Marx
The Socialist Tradition in the French Revolution
Authority in the Modern State
The Problem of Sovereignty
Political thought in England
Communism
The Dangers of Obedience
The Communist Manifesto: Socialist Landmark
An American Democracy
Trade Unions in the New Society

HAROLD J. LASKI

AN INTRODUCTION TO POLITICS

H. J. Laski

LONDON · UNWIN BOOKS

First Published in May 1931
Second Impression October 1931
Third Impression 1932
Fourth Impression 1934
Fifth Impression 1936
Sixth Impression 1939
Seventh Impression 1943
Eighth Impression 1945
Revised Edition (Ninth Impression) 1951
Tenth Impression 1954
Eleventh Impression 1958
First Published in this Edition 1961
Second Impression 1962
Third Impression 1963
Fourth Impression 1966
Fifth Impression 1968

*This book is copyright under the Berne Convention.
Apart from any fair dealing for the purposes of
private study, research, criticism or review, as permitted under the Copyright Act 1956, no portion
may be reproduced by any process without written
permission. Enquiries should be addressed to the
publisher.*

UNWIN BOOKS

*George Allen & Unwin Ltd
Ruskin House Museum Street
London*

Cloth edition SBN 04 320019 2
Paper edition SBN 04 320020 6

PRINTED IN GREAT BRITAIN
in 10 *point Plantin type*
BY C. TINLING AND CO LTD
LIVERPOOL, LONDON AND PRESCOT

TO JAN AND TONIA

Professor Laski wrote this book in 1930 *not only as a popular introduction to the subject but also as an encouragement to the average reader to explore the classical texts, or even his own fuller exposition,* Grammar of Politics.

It was revised and brought up to date in the spirit of the original edition in 1951 *by Martin Wight, with the help of Ralph Miliband, a friend and colleague of Professor Laski, and Geoffrey Goodwin.*

CONTENTS

CHAPTER ONE

The Nature of the State

I

EVERY citizen of the modern world is the subject of a state. He is legally bound to obey its orders, and the contours of his life are set by the norms that it imposes. These norms are the law, and it is in the power to enforce them upon all who live within its boundaries that the essence of the state is to be found. For whereas all other associations are voluntary in character, and can bind the individual only as he chooses membership of them, once he is a resident of some given state, legally he has no choice but to obey its commands. These are superior in their legal claim to the demand upon him of any alternative body. The state, so to say, is the crowning-point of the modern social edifice, and it is in its supremacy over all other forms of social grouping that its special nature is to be found.

The state is thus a way of regulating human conduct. Any analysis of its character reveals it as a method of imposing principles of behaviour by which men must regulate their lives. The state orders us not to steal; it punishes us for a violation of its order. It lays down a system of imperatives, and uses coercion to secure obedience to them. From its own standpoint, the validity of those imperatives is self-derived. They are legal, not because they are good, or just, or wise, but because they are its imperatives. They are the legal expression of the way in which men should act as laid down by the authority which is alone competent to make final decisions of this kind.

But legal imperatives neither state themselves nor are self-enforced. They have been willed by some man, or some body of men, and by some man or some body of men they must be enforced. When we examine the states of the modern world, we find that they always present the spectacle of a large number of men obeying, within a defined territory, a small number of other men. We find, also, that the rules made by this small number, whether, as in Great Britain, they are omnicompetent (the King in Parliament) or, as in the United States, are limited both as to the subject-matter about which they can command obedience and the methods by which this is achieved, nevertheless possess this quality that, should they be violated, this small number of men can use all the coercion that is necessary to vindicate their authority. Every state, in short, is a territorial society divided into government and subjects, the government being a body of persons within the state who apply the legal imperatives upon which the state rests; and, differently from any other body of persons within the territorial society, they are entitled to use coercion to see that these imperatives are obeyed.

In every state, this is to say, there is a will which is legally pre-eminent over all other wills. It makes the final determinations of the society. It is, in the technical phrase, a sovereign will. It neither receives orders from any other will, nor can it finally alienate its authority. Such a will, for example, is that of the King in Parliament in Great Britain. Within the confines of its territory, whatever it decides is binding upon all residents within that territory. They may consider its decisions immoral or unwise; they are nevertheless legally bound to obey them. A British subject who disliked some decision of his church might leave his church; it would be unable to enforce his acceptance of its decision. But a British subject who disliked the law relating to the income-tax would nevertheless be legally bound to obey it. His attempt to challenge its efficacy would be met at once by compulsory subjection, in one form or another, to its consequences.

The state is thus a society of individuals submitted, if necessary, by compulsion, to a certain way of life. All conduct in the society must conform to that way. The rules which settle its character are the laws of the state, and, by an obvious logic, they have necessary primacy, are, that is to say, sovereign, over all other rules. In this society, the individuals who make and enforce the rules are termed the government; and that portion of the rules which settles (*a*) how such rules are to be made (*b*) the manner in which they are to be changed (*c*) who are to make them, is called the constitution of the state.

II

This is, of course, to view the state as a purely legal order. It is simply a description of the way in which social relationships are geared together in a modern community, without regard either to the way in which the present system has developed, the purposes that it serves, or the value and dangers which attach to it as it functions.

Obviously enough, all of these are important. The character of the modern state is the consequence of the history through which it has passed, and it would be unintelligible save in the light of that history. The power of the state is not exerted in a vacuum. It is used to achieve certain ends, and its rules are, in their substance, altered to secure the ends deemed good at some particular time by those in possession of the legal right to operate its power. Our sense, again, of the value and dangers of the state as thus conceived will clearly depend very largely upon our view of the ends it is seeking to serve, and the way in which it seeks to serve them.

With the history of the state I cannot here pretend to deal. It must be sufficient only to emphasise that its character as a sovereign body was the product of a long chain of historical circumstances of which the most important was the need, at the time of the Reformation, to find a plane of organisation to which all claims to authority could be referred for ultimate decisions. The state secured its primacy over all other associations because, at that period, it offered prospects of ordered peace such as no other body could pretend to secure. The anarchy of religious faiths seemed to promise little save conflict; economic organisation was too local and atomistic in character to be capable of making general rules. The state emerged as the one association capable of laying down legal imperatives which the mass of men would respect. It was able to order life because, without its commands, there would have been no order. Its triumph was inherent in its ability to enforce its will upon all men against competitors who strove not less ardently for their allegiance.

Why was it able to enforce its will? At this point, we pass from the nature of the state viewed as a purely legal order, to the state as a subject of philosophic analysis. Here, clearly, we must look at it from two different angles. We have to explain what the purposes of the state seem, in general fact, to be: what, that is, explains the character of the legal imperatives it imposes at any given time. We have, also, to search for criteria which will enable us to determine what, again in general terms, the character of those legal imperatives ought to be. What, in a word, explains the habits of some given state, say those of the France of the *ancien régime*? What causes us to make the judgment that the French state of the *ancien régime* was inadequate, in its operation, to the purposes for which a state should exist?

The authority of a state is a function of its ability to satisfy the effective demands that are made upon it. Its subjects desire, for instance, security for their persons and property. The legal imperatives of a state are then directed to satisfying that desire. Its subjects wish to worship God in their own way, without the imposition of prohibitions upon any particular form of religious belief. If the demand cannot be gainsaid, the state makes religious toleration one of its legal imperatives. The reason for the French Revolution was simply that, under the system of legal imperatives maintained by the *ancien régime*, it was impossible to satisfy the demands made upon the institutions of the state by its members.

Legal imperatives, that is to say, are a function of effective demand. They will correspond to the desires of those who know how to make their wishes felt at the centre of political power. The laws of any given state will be an effort to respond to those desires; and their efficacy will depend upon the degree to which that response is successful. From, that is, the vast and competing welter of desires which the state confronts among its members, some, and not others, are selected for translation into legally imperative terms. The principle of selection is not a constant one; either time or place determines its operation. We cannot conceive a state in Western civilisation which does not tax its members to support a system of national education. Yet, less than a century and a half ago it would have been unthinkable that any state should have compelled its members to contribute to such a purpose. A demand which was then ineffective has become, in the process of time, irresistible.

Why? Clearly, because those who exercise the authority of the state have judged it necessary, or wise, or just, to yield to a demand for a national system of education. But we have to discover what it is which makes such a demand effective at a given time and place. The answer, obviously, cannot be that the demand was reasonable: the state has often refused effect to reasonable demands, and accepted those which, on their face, reason could never justify. Nor can it be the wisdom of their substance, since statesmen do not always act wisely. Necessity is a more obvious cause; but we then need to know why one demand is, at some given time and place, deemed necessary by the state, and not another.

The motives, doubtless, which lead statesmen to action are far too complicated to permit of simple explanation; no one cause is finally exclusive of others. Yet it may be taken as a general rule that the character of any particular state will be, broadly speaking, a function of the economic system which obtains in the society it controls. Any social system reveals itself as a struggle for the control of economic power, since those who possess this power are able, in the measure of their possession, to make their wants effective. Law then becomes a system of relations giving the expression of legal form to their wants. The way, therefore, in which economic power is distributed at any given time and place will shape the character of the legal imperatives which are imposed in that same time and place. The state, in these circumstances, expresses the wants of those who dominate the economic system. The legal order is a mask behind which a dominant economic interest secures the benefits of political authority. The state, as it operates, does not deliberately seek general justice, or general utility, but the interest, in the largest sense, of the dominant class in society.

We must be careful not to read into this view either more than it means or more than it can justify. It explains the general character of a state; it does not explain the details of its actions. It argues broadly that privilege usually goes with the possession of property, and that exclusion from property will be exclusion from privilege. It argues that as the balance of ownership is altered in a society, so the balance of state-action will alter to meet the new equilibrium. That alteration, of course, is rarely immediate, and never complete; there is a time-lag in historic movements which makes all adaptation partial. Few classes which have attained power ever utilise it in an extreme way. They have to purchase the consent of their opponents to the new equilibrium; and they will themselves not seldom feel that their own admission to power is in itself satisfactory without an effort at that exclusiveness from which they had previously suffered. But no one who studies the legislation of a state can doubt its relativity to the demands of the class which acts in its name. The history of trade-union law in England, of freedom of contract in America, of agrarian legislation in Prussia, are all instances of the way in which a dominant economic class uses the state to make ultimate those legal imperatives which best protect its interests.

This is not to deny for one moment a desire in the governing class to act reasonably or justly. But men think differently who live differently; and in the approach to the problem of what legal imperatives are ultimately desirable in the interests of the community as a whole, each class approaches the question with an unstated and half-conscious major premise at the back of its mind which is of fundamental importance to its view of reason or justice. Rich men always underestimate the power of property to secure happiness; religious men always over-estimate the influence of faith upon morals; learned men usually attach undue importance to the relation of scholarship to wisdom. We are the prisoners of our experience; and since the main item in our experience is gained in the effort to make our living, the way in which that living is earned is that which most profoundly shapes our notions of what is desirable. John Bright could never see the value of Factory Acts because, as an employer, they contradicted the experience he had most keenly felt; and a landowner like Lord Shaftesbury, who had no difficulty in seeing the elementary justice of factory legislation, could never see the justice of regulating the conditions of agricultural labour. The slave-owners of the Confederate states believed in all sincerity that a system of slavery was in the interest of the slaves themselves.

It is sometimes said that this theory may hold of a community in which power is oligarchical in character; an England, for example, in which the franchise is confined to the middle class, naturally promotes legislation of a predominantly middle-class character. But where the state is a democracy based upon universal suffrage, the fact that the governors of the state are chosen by the community as a whole makes an economic interpretation obsolete which rests upon the theory that the power of property mainly determines its character.

The objection, however, is less substantial than appears upon the surface. It is true that a democratic state will be, in general, more generous to the multitude than an oligarchical state; the difference between English legislation in the nineteenth and the twentieth centuries makes this self-evident. But those differences do not touch the root of the matter. Power depends for its habits upon a consciousness of possession, a habit of organization, an ability to produce an immediate effect. In a democratic state, where there are great inequalities of economic power, the main characteristics of the poor are exactly the want of these. They do not know the power that they possess. They hardly realise what can be effected by organising their interests. They lack direct access to those who govern them. Any action by the working-classes, even in a democratic state, involves risk to their economic security out of all proportion to the certainty of gain. They have rarely in their hands the instruments necessary to secure their desires. They have seldom even learned how these may best be formulated and defended. They labour under the sense of inferiority which comes from perpetual obedience to orders without any full experience of the confidence which comes from the habit of command. They tend to confound the institutions they have inherited with the inescapable foundations of society. There is, in fact, every reason to expect that a state built upon universal suffrage will be responsible for wider concessions to the multitude than will be granted under any alternative form; but there is no historic reason to suppose that such a state will be able of itself directly to alter at the root the social results of an economically unequal society.

We conclude, that is, that the nature of the legal imperatives in any given state corresponds to the effective demands that state encounters, and that these, in their turn, depend, in a general way, upon the manner in which economic power is distributed in the society which that state controls. It then follows that the more equally economic power is distributed, the profounder will be the relation between the general interest of the community and the legal imperatives imposed by the state. For, obviously, equal economic power means equal effective demand; and the will of the state is then not specially biased in one direction rather than in another. And if the state is an organisation for giving effect to demand, the more equally distributed the power that it encounters, the more total will be its response.

That, at any rate, seems the general experience of history. The aristocratic state has endured because the number of those excluded from its benefits who were conscious of their power to challenge its foundations was too small to be effective; and it has perished because a change in the system of production has so altered the incidence of property in that state that those excluded from power have been able, if they shared effectively in the new scheme of things, to force an extension to their own benefit of the legal imperatives which the state imposed.

At this point, then, we are in a position to judge the meaning of the state regarded purely as a legal order. So to regard it tells us nothing of its validity beyond the legal sphere. The state as a system of legal imperatives is a temporary parallelogram of forces the character of which shifts as the forces alter which determine its momentary position. Its laws are valid only in the sense that, at some given moment, they can, in fact, be imposed. Once they are urged as valid on grounds other than the fact of their ultimate source, we move beyond the sphere of law into realms where other factors obtain. An act of Congress or Parliament, that is, presses for acceptance in the legal sphere merely because it is an act of Congress or Parliament. If it seeks acceptance upon other grounds, because, for example, it is wise, or just, the source from which it emanates is, upon this footing, irrelevant. For it is then presenting itself in terms of a theory of value the justification for which cannot be found in the pure realm of law.

III

There comes into view here the second aspect of the philosophy of the state to which I have already referred. We have described the state as, in law, a system of imperatives imposed in its name by a body of men, who, in their corporate aspect, are termed the government. We have seen that the system of imperatives derives its substantial character from the economic system which, at any given time, underlies that legal order which expresses the incidence of effective demand in the society. Obviously, this tells us nothing outside the realm of pure fact. It explains why a state embarks upon legislation of a special character. It does not explain what character should attach to the legislation of the state as such.

A theory of pure law, that is, presents itself for acceptance on the ground of the source from which it derives. But if I ask why I should be expected to obey the state, it is clearly not sufficient to tell me that I must obey it because it is the state. I shall ask, as men in the past have asked, why the dictates of the state deserve obedience; and if those dictates contradict all that I think and hope and feel, I may well conclude, as men in the past have concluded, that I have no alternative open to me but to refuse the obedience thus demanded of me.

The commands of the state, therefore, must justify themselves on grounds other than their source in the fiat of the state. Such origin tells us where they come from; it tells us that coercion to obey will, as a rule, be at their disposal. But it tells us no more. It does not tell us that the state was justified in making these commands. A legal theory of the state is thus not a theory of right until it is more than a theory of law. We have to enquire what law is for, what ends it represents itself as serving, why it considers that those ends ought to be our ends, before we have a theory of the state which can be regarded as adequate for the purpose of political philosophy. We have to add, so to say, a teleology to law in order to commend it to the acceptance of men.

Teleologies of law are almost as various as the historic experience of mankind. But it is worth while to distinguish certain outstanding conceptions in order to see how men have sought to justify the institutional systems under which they have lived. In the early experience of mankind, the most general view may be termed the theological. Law is a body of divine rules given to those who live under them by a god or gods, and worthy, accordingly, of obedience because of their divine inspiration. Such, clearly, was the law of Moses, or that code of Hammurabi which the sun-god gave him in complete detail. Men are asked to obey them because divine anger will follow their infraction. Or, at one remove from this, we may have law as a body of ancient customs, not perhaps written, but traditionally preserved by a priestly caste, and demanding the obedience of men through fear of divine displeasure if they are broken.

Such theories, for the most part, belong to the primitive history of mankind. In a more mature period, that, for example, of Roman jurisprudence, obedience to law is recommended essentially on the ground that its priciples are born of the ultimate nature of things, and that men's behaviour ought, accordingly, to conform to them. Such a cosmological view is akin to that of Thomas Aquinas. For him law is a mirror wherein is reflected the divine reason which planned and governs the universe. In obeying it, as men ought to obey it, they are clearly bringing their conduct into accord with the plan upon which the good order of the world depends. Analogous, again, is the view taken by Kant which looks upon law as a system of precepts enabling each individual to realise his greatest freedom consistently with a like freedom in other individuals. This view becomes a cosmology with Hegel when the process of history is made an idea of the unfolding of an ever greater freedom which realises itself in the evolution of the state.

All such theories have one characteristic; they place the sanction of law outside the control of men. Whether it is the fear of God, or the realisation of the plan inherent in the universe, or the attainment of increasing freedom, they do not conceive of man as an independent factor whose own experience deliberately and consciously shapes the making of law. Its substance, so to speak, is always 'out there', to be found by him; goodness consists in conformity with a code he has had no hand in making. He is asked to take a body of precepts upon trust as embodying the inescapable results of the world-process, or, at least, results from which he escapes at the peril of his salvation.

It is plain enough that such theories will not do. Historical research has shattered all systems which claim to operate under theological sanctions; the God of their revelations speaks the language of a mystery which has no magic save for his self-appointed votaries. Those, moreover, based upon the supposed logic of a world-process which is the voice of nature or of reason are obviously derived from an attempt to discover in the social world laws analogous in character to those of inanimate nature. The attempt is impossible. It neglects the fact that the social world is not only permanently dynamic but also permanently novel; the factors in its equations are the active wills of individual men who, by scrutinising the contingent results, are in a position to change them. They make change by willing change. Laws, therefore, which have the tough constancy of natural laws, those, for example, of physics and chemistry, are impossible of attainment in the political realm. A social life according to nature, as in the Stoic ideal, forgets that in a civilised world art is man's nature; and a life according to the highest principles of art depends upon a view of beauty or goodness which can claim universal application.

Now the fact is that most of the theories of law we have just considered have always justified a social order in which the many lived for the benefit of the few; it is hardly a caricature of Hegel's theory of the state, for example, to say that, for him, man found the highest expression of his freedom in obedience to the King of Prussia. Such views, in a word, have been the imposition of conceptions derived from a partial and biased experience upon the wills of the rest of the community, without any adequate attempt to elicit from others how far their experience conformed with the result of such conceptions. This it is which has given its attractiveness to a theory of law which, from the time of ancient Greece, has exercised a perennial fascination over men.

The theory, in its elements at least, is a simple one. Law, it argues, cannot be binding upon men unless they consent to make it so. The factor, therefore, which gives to the legal imperatives of any system of state their validity is the fact that men have agreed to the underlying principles upon which they are built. Everyone knows that life is impossible unless men keep their promises: let us found the state upon consent, and the laws which the state makes may then claim to bind its citizens. Otherwise, obviously, it is naked coercion, and cannot be given any ethical foundation.

This, in its cruder forms, is the theory of a social contract. Men agree, it is said, to make the state and endow it with the power to issue orders. Sometimes, as with Hobbes, the power is unlimited and irrevocable; to escape from the horrors of anarchy men give themselves a despot as master. Sometimes, as with Locke, the power is, on the contrary, limited and revocable; men see the advantage of a state, but they do not agree to make it omnicompetent. It must be equated with a limited company and, at the peril of revolution, live strictly within its memorandum of association. Sometimes, finally, as with Rousseau, the state emerges from the consent of men as omnicompetent; but, as it acts, each of their wills forms at each stage of action a part of its will. The state is conducted by permanent referendum, and its law binds its members because they are themselves making its substance.

No one, I think, can deny that theories which justify the claim of the law to obedience in terms of consent have a strength behind them to which no rival view can pretend. In their terms, the individual, by consenting to the law, makes his own obligation, and it is thus obviously reasonable that he should thus regard himself as bound. But we must not omit the grave defects from which such theories suffer. We have no evidence of an original social contract such as the theory demands; the state has not been made, but has grown. Nor could its operations be conducted upon the basis of consent alone. There is not only the fact that, at some point, a dissenting minority must be made to give way; there is also the fact that once we pass beyond the small city-state, the problem of size makes representative government, in some shape, the only form through which it is practicable for the will of the state to find expression. The advocates of a contractual theory often speak at this point of a tacit consent; but it is clear that because consent involves the notion of a deliberate act of will, something more positive than this is required. And what are we to say of law to which a man consents when it is made, and, later, after experience of its operation, withdraws his consent? Is it still valid for him? Would not the power to revoke consent make the business of administration impossible? Clearly, while any system of legal imperatives is better in the degree that it involves a minimum of coercion, it is impossible to think of a modern community the ends of which can be obtained without the exercise of force over some, at least, of its citizens.

IV

Let us put our central problem in another way. The state, I have said, is a way of regulating human conduct. It is a legal order the norms of which bind the behaviour of men in one way, rather than other. Its action is ultimately imperative action which none of its citizens is legally entitled to escape. Why does it possess this power? It is difficult to see an explanation in other than functional terms. The power of the state can be justified only in terms of what it seeks to do. Its law must be capable of justification in terms of the demands it seeks to satisfy. The state presides over a vast welter of interests, personal and corporate, competing and co-operating. Its claim to allegiance must obviously be built upon its power to make the response to social demand maximal in character. It must strike such a balance of interests that what emerges as satisfied is greater than can be secured on any alternative programme. How exactly the balance is to be struck we cannot say on any permanent principle, simply because each age will value things differently, and an absolute formula of intrinsic worth will be obsolete as soon as it is made. We can only argue that legal imperatives may be imposed if, in their operation, we satisfy at the least sacrifice as much as we can of human want. We have then to shape the institutions through which the state operates in order that it may best attain this end.

CHAPTER TWO

The Place of the State in the Great Society

I

I HAVE argued that the power of the state is justified to the degree that it secures, at the least possible sacrifice, the maximum satisfaction of human wants; and the quality with which it performs this function alone gives it a title to an allegiance other than purely formal.

Properly to appreciate what this implies we must understand the place of the state in the great society. It is, I have said, a way of regulating human behaviour; clearly, the regulations must be justified by their results in the lives of individual members of the state. Each of these finds himself seeking happiness by way of a constant effort to fulfil his desires. The state, for him, is the supreme body laying down the rules within which he must act as he strives for that fulfilment. Some of its imperatives he may approve, others he may bitterly dislike. The state, that is, may sin for him either by way of omission or commission. He is seeking to affect the substance of its will by making it, as best he can, accord with the lesson of his own experience.

For the individual is not merely a member of the state. In the society of which he is a part, there are innumerable interest-units to which he may belong. He is a member of a church, an ardent trade-unionist, a keen freemason, a zealous supporter of a movement for compulsory vaccination, a pacifist to whom a conscientious objection to military service is the central principle of life. He is, so to say, interstitially connected with associations seeking to promote each of these interests. They live, for the most part, within the ambit of the rules which the state lays down. Its will settles the boundaries within which their wills, as associations, must operate. Their wills bind their members, in law, only to the point of accordance with the legal imperatives which the state lays down.

But because the individual is not merely a member of the state, he does not feel obliged to obey it merely because it is, legally, the sovereign organisation of society. His own experience counts. He judges what the state does. There is in him an Athanasius-element which makes him apart from, as well as one with, its actions. If his church conflicts with the state, he chooses, and he alone can choose, where his allegiance should go. If the state decides to repress his trade-union he helps to decide whether the repression shall be accepted. The state, so to say, acts always in an atmosphere of contingency. Successfully to coerce, it must be able successfully to persuade. It must make him feel that his good is bound up with the legal imperatives that it is trying to establish. It wins his allegiance not by being the state, but because of what, as the state, it is seeking to do.

Normally, perhaps, we hardly see the contingent character of the state's claim to obedience because, normally, the individual does not hesitate to obey. The power of the state is immense; the challenge it must offer to the individual must go to the roots of his being before he feels the call to attack its authority. But anyone who considers the normal history of the nationalist movements, or the lives of revolutionary leaders and the parties they direct, or of agitations like that for women's suffrage in England before 1914, will see that where the habits of the state outrage the individual's sense of right, he, and those who think with him, are prepared, in the last analysis, to register dissent from its activities.

Nor can we condemn their dissent without committing ourselves to the principle that order is the highest good in

society. That is, surely, an impossible view. Order is good for
what it implies and not for its own sake. To preserve order
where the activities of the state are a perpetual outrage to its
citizens is surely to sacrifice all that makes life worth living.
We give, that is to say, our allegiance to the state always upon
the condition that its end, as a state, satisfies the end we set
before ourselves. Its sovereignty is contingent upon our agreement to its exercise. As it operates, it must leave us with a sense
that our good is involved in the attainment of its good. We must
feel that the rules it lays down are not less the conditions of our
happiness than of those of other members of the state. Where it
so acts as to contradict the burden of our experience, we are
driven to the necessity of challenge, if we can make that challenge
effective.

Let us put this in another way. The state maintains its rules
not for the sake of the rules, but for what they do to individual
lives. Each of its members is striving to be happy. He then needs
the conditions without which happiness is unattainable; and he
judges the state by its ability to secure those conditions for
him. Obviously enough, the state cannot guarantee happiness
to everyone, for the simple reason that some of the conditions
of happiness are beyond its control. A man may feel that life is
not worth living without the love of some particular woman;
but no one would argue that he was entitled to expect from the
state the assurance of her love. All that we can say is that there
are, at least, certain general conditions of happiness, affecting
all citizens alike, which are the minimum bases of a satisfactory
social life. These, at the least, the state must secure to its
members, if it is to count upon their continuous obedience to
its rules.

The rules, in a word, that the state lays down imply claims
against the state. For what the state can do is obviously limited
by its end; and that end involves rights for the citizen against
the state in order that the end may be safeguarded. What do we

mean by the idea of rights ? It is a condition without which, in the light of historic experience, the individual lacks assurance that he can attain happiness. We cannot, that is, say that the rights of the individual are constant; they are obviously relative to time and place. But, granted that relativity, the individual is entitled to expect their recognition from the state as the condition of his obedience to its commands.

The best way, perhaps, to see what this implies is to picture to ourselves the position of the normal citizen in a society like our own. He cannot expect happiness without personal security; he must know, as an ordinary and expected condition of life, that he is safe from personal attack. He must have the means of living, and this means a recognition of either the right to work, or, in its absence, of a decent maintenance by society. But the right to work, barely stated, does not meet the wants of civilised living. It must mean, therefore, the right to work at a reasonable wage, and for such hours of labour as enable him to attain significance for himself beyond the getting of his livelihood. I say a reasonable wage: by which I mean such payment as secures the satisfaction of normal physical appetite and does not prevent the satisfaction of the more spiritual demands of men. I argue that there is a right to reasonable hours of labour because in a civilisation like our own, which is dominated by machine technology, most citizens must find their main fulfilment of personality in the hours of leisure and not of toil. A state which permitted the employer to exact from them the kind of unremitting effort characteristic of the early days of the Industrial Revolution would frustrate for them the possibility of attaining happiness. The right to leisure, therefore, is one of the legal imperatives upon which a well-ordered state must insist.

But the individual needs more than this if his happiness is to be certain of consideration in the state. He must know his relationship to other men, and be able to report the meaning of his experience of that relation. To this end knowledge is essential, and the right to education is therefore fundamental to citizenship. For without education, at least as a general rule, a man is lost in a big world he is unable to understand. He cannot make the most of himself; he cannot be critical about the meaning of experience. The uneducated man amid the complexities of modern civilisation is like a blind man who cannot relate cause and effect. The state which denies education to its citizens denies them the means of realising their personality.

But education alone is not enough. It may confer knowledge upon a citizen to whom the state yet denies the opportunity of using his knowledge. And since a denial of the right to use is, in general, a denial of the right to benefit, it is necessary to safeguard the citizen on this head. To this end, four rights are essential. He must be able freely to speak his mind; he must have the right to associate with others like-minded with himself for the promotion of some end, or ends, upon which they are agreed; he must be able to assist in choosing those by whom he is to be governed; and he must be able, if he can persuade others to choose him, himself to take a part in the governance of the state.

Effectively, this is to say that no state will realise the end for which it exists unless it is a democracy based upon universal suffrage in which there are not only freedom of speech and association, but also a recognition that neither race nor creed, birth nor property, shall be a barrier against the exercise of civic rights. We have to assume this simply because it is the experience of history that the exclusion of any group of men from power is, sooner or later, their exclusion from the benefits of power. The will of the state is always operated by a government in terms of the wants of those upon whom that government depends for the refreshment of its authority. To make the area of dependence coincident with the whole citizen body is, therefore, to maximise the possibility that the totality of wants will be considered. We need not deny that there are difficulties inherent in a democratic system; but no philosophy of politics can seriously claim to satisfy the demands of the individual unless it bases itself upon a recognition that citizens are equally entitled to the satisfaction of their desires. And the only way in which their desires can affect the will of the state with continuous emphasis is when the government of the state is compelled, by constitutional principle, to take them into definite account.

A word is necessary about freedom of speech and association. Nothing is more urgent in a state than men should be able both freely to speak their minds about its problems, and that they should be able to act freely together in pursuit of objects upon which they are agreed. If these are penalised, we may be certain that the results of experience will be denied. The state will suppress uncomfortable opinion, and it will prevent the organisation of voluntary bodies which seek for ends it does not appreciate. Because experience is different, the right to pursue its consequences is fundamental to self-realisation. Indeed, it may be said with truth that the condition of a state can rarely be better measured than by its tolerance of ideas different from, or opposed to, the legal imperatives it seeks to impose. Every effort at suppression is, in fact, an attempt to refuse the satisfaction of desire. It is an attempt to limit the experience which is to count. It tilts the incidence of state-action to the benefit of a part only of the community.

We cannot, however, say that the right to these freedoms is unlimited. The state must, because its business is the preservation of order, concern itself to see that the peace is maintained. It is, therefore, entitled to say that any utterance which directly incites to immediate disorder is subject to penalty; and that any association which embarks upon action likely to threaten the maintenance of order shall, also, be subject to penalty. On this head, for example, it could never suppress a book or pamphlet; but it could penalise an orator, say in Trafalgar Square, who urged an excited mob to march upon Downing Street. It could not suppress a society of Tolstoyan anarchists because, by definition, their principles are incompatible with violence; but it would be entitled to suppress a body which, like the Ulster Volunteers, deliberately organised itself to resist by force the legal imperatives of the state. The limits of freedom are always set by the imminence of a threat to social peace. Where there is no such urgency, interference by the state is a denial of right.

Nor must we neglect that body of rights which look to the protection of the interests of personality. A man is entitled to such religious faith as he pleases to profess; and so long as the behaviour connected with its expression does not directly threaten the public peace the state has no right to interfere. He is entitled, also, to full judicial protection. Things like double jeopardy, or the *ex post facto* definition of crime in order to secure penalties against an individual, the search of his house without a duly executed warrant, a level of court costs which makes access to the Courts practically impossible for the poor, all these are instances of action which deny the realisation of right to the individual. The interests of personality, moreover, demand one definite limitation upon freedom of speech. I should not, without penalty, be permitted to speak scandal of my neighbour unless I can show (1) that the accusation made is true, and (2) that it is in the common interest that it should be made public.

II

Such a system of rights is necessary in the state in order that the citizen may be assured of adequate treatment. Without them, he will not be free; without them, that is, he will find that the limitations upon the expression of his personality hinder fatally the prospect of its self-realisation. Nor can he hope, unless such rights are general, to be assured of equal consideration with other men. Where, in any society, those who enjoy rights such as these are limited in number, whatever be the principle of limitation, it will be found that its consequence is a limitation to those who are privileged of the benefits of state-action.

Underlying this conception of rights is the thesis that no citizen is more entitled than any other, merely as a citizen, to response to his demands. Any system of legal imperatives which results in differential advantage to some body of citizens is an invasion of the purpose of the state, a denial of its end, unless it can be shown that there is a direct and causal relationship between such differential advantage and the well-being of the society as a whole. In so far, that is, as the state protects differences of satisfaction in response to demand, it must be able to show that these differences are demanded by the common good.

No one, in fact, can analyse the conditions of modern social life without being impressed by the different returns made to individual demand. There is no proportion between effort and reward. There is little attempt to equalise the security which is conferred by the state on its citizens. As its legal imperatives work, they tend to protect existing possession of privilege rather than to extend it. The division of society into rich and poor makes the legal imperatives of the state work to the advantage of the rich. And this is to say that the effect of the system of property under which we live is to bias the interpretation of the legal imperatives which control men's lives. It makes the power of demand so different in the different classes of society that, in Disraeli's famous phrase, they seem to belong rather to two nations than to the same people.

The inference which political philosophy must draw from this situation is the impossibility of maintaining the end of the state if there are great material differences in the position of citizens. A nation divided into rich and poor is as a house divided against itself. Wealth breeds arrogance, as poverty breeds inferiority. A wealthy class strives, inevitably, to protect its advantages at their maximum; and the poor are driven to attempt their invasion as the only way of enjoying their results. The state, therefore, is compelled, if it seeks to realise its end, so to organise its activities as deliberately to mitigate the consequences of this material inequality. It has, by the use of the taxing-power, to hold the rich to ransom, in the effort to satisfy the demands of the poor. Anyone who observes the way in which, during the last fifty years, the police-state of the nineteenth century has been transformed into the social service state of the twentieth will realise how inequality is only able to maintain itself by acquiescence in concessions, for which it has to pay. And these concessions grow in volume. For every improvement in education, or health, or housing among the poor leads to an increased intensity of demand for further concessions. They realise the inadequacy of a social system which does not relate proportionately the toil and the gain of living. The passion for equality, in a word, is a permanent feature of human nature. No state is secure save as it organises the satisfaction of this sentiment; it may postpone, but it cannot avoid, the effort to convince its members that its legal imperatives, not merely in form, but also in substance, represent the general attainment of justice.

Here we must advance certain propositions which follow upon the view of rights discussed a little earlier. No system of legal imperatives maintains itself. Day by day it has to be applied to different, and, often, novel, situations. Now it is a commonplace of philosophy that those who execute measures are in fact their masters. Legal imperatives have to be interpreted. Where the line of free speech must be drawn; when, exactly, an association threatens the peaceful life of society; whether a piece of legislation is desirable or undesirable; whether an inference, for example, from the nature of trade-unions is their right to secure parliamentary representation; whether, as in the United States, the limitation of the hours of labour is a violation of the general principle that liberty of contract is desirable; decisions upon these, and a host of similar issues have to be made. Each involves a balancing of interests in the society, and it is clearly of the first importance to be clear how that balance is made.

What occurs in any state where there are great material differences between classes is simply a perversion of the end of the state to the interests of the rich. Their power compels the agents of the state to make their wishes the first object of consideration. Their conception of good insensibly pervades the mental climate of administration. They dominate the machinery of the state. By justice they mean the satisfaction of their demands. By the lessons of history they mean the deposit of their experience. Anyone who considers for example, the history of the interpretation of trade-union law by the judges in England, especially as manifested in such a decision as the famous Osborne case, will find it difficult to avoid the conclusion that the judicial mind of a middle-class state is unable to penetrate the needs of the working-class. Anyone who, in the United States, takes the history of the Fourteenth Amendment can hardly help insisting that the Courts have been the instrument of business men in their fight against the development of social legislation. And the history of the establishment of the Fascist regime in Italy, the Nazi tyranny in Germany and the Franco dictatorship in Spain is the record of a deliberate alteration of the whole constitutional arrangements of the state, encouraged and supported by the employers' class because it would involve, among much else, the destruction of trade-union organisation. Here we have seen a naked perversion of democratic machinery, achieved by force.

I conclude that the end of the state cannot be realised where

C

the power to make the demand effective is seriously different among its members; and such difference is a matter of economic arrangement. From this angle, the legal imperatives of the state have, as they operate, no rightness about them that is other than purely formal. Each individual, and each group of individuals, is fully entitled to make up his mind about their validity, and to act upon the results of that judgment.

From this there follows a theory of law which is of the first importance for political philosophy. Law appears as the registration of that will in society which has known how to make itself effective. It has no claim to obedience merely because it is effective. Its claim to obedience depends upon what it does to the lives of individual citizens. Of this result they alone can judge; and the rightness of law, therefore, depends upon their judgment of it. Any state, therefore, is bound by the nature of its end so to organise its institutions that the judgment of its citizens upon its legal imperatives may be made fully known, and equally weighed. For, otherwise, its consequences are not adequately discovered. The response it makes is limited to satisfying the wants of powerful citizens; and, in so far as their experience represents an interest different from the rest of the community, it follows that the response is based to their advantage. The only claim, in such circumstances, that the state can make to obedience is built upon the chaos which results from a challenge to its authority. That claim, we may grant, is a powerful one. Resistance ought always, from the cost it involves, to be a weapon of last instance. But on the view here taken it is impossible to argue that it should not be used. The right to resist the law is the reserve-power in society by which men whose demands are denied may legitimately seek to alter the balance of forces in the state.

Law, therefore, is a claim to obedience validated by experience of its results. There is no inherent difference between its claim and that of a rule drawn from experience by the individual himself or by an association of individuals except the force applied by the state to get obedience to its commands. The sanction of the rules made by the state is simply force; and force in itself is void of moral content. Where a state is in conflict, therefore, with a church, or a trade-union, or a body like the Communist Party, it has no *a priori* claim to allegiance. Its claim depends upon the view taken of the conflict by those who are related to it. The state is only entitled to victory as it proves to its citizens that its laws must result for them in lives of fuller substance. Its sovereignty is a function of the quality of the life that it makes for its members.

III

Objections are made against this view on various grounds. It is not, it is said, a neat theory which presents a fully co-ordinated pattern of social institutions. Not only does it leave room for anarchy; it even pretends that there are occasions when anarchy is justified. While it agrees that, as a legal order, the state is sovereign, it proceeds at once to deprive that sovereignty of anything more than purely formal significance. It makes the state, in fact, compete for the allegiance of citizens with all other associations in society; and where there is conflict between them, it gives to the state no assurance of victory. It completely separates the law of the state from justice; and while it defines the philosophic purpose of the state, it refuses to see that purpose as inherent in its operation.

I do not deny that the theory here set forth gives ground for all the objections I have enumerated. But are any of them important? Life, after all, is too complex and various a thing for all its manifestations to be capable of reduction to a single formula. There is bound to be at least the prospect of anarchy in the state so long as men move differently to the attainment of opposed desires; and no one can say that a refusal to obey the state is always incapable of justification. It is true that, upon this theory, the sovereignty of the state is no more than a formal source of reference. But it is surely impossible to regard it otherwise without ascribing to it a permanent wisdom in all its operations which is directly at variance with our experience of them. It is true, also, that the state is made here to compete for the allegiance of citizens with all other associations in society. But, once more, is it not in fact obvious that it does so compete? Anyone who considers the history of conflicts like that between Bismarck and the Roman Catholic Church, between Sinn Fein and the British government, between Austria and its Italian citizens during the Risorgimento, or, as a final instance, between Tsarist Russia and the revolutionary associations, will find it difficult indeed to argue that the state has ever lived, or can ever live, upon other terms, so long as its members have demands which remain unsatisfied. And the experience of prohibition in America makes it strikingly clear that the state cannot hope for an adequate enforcement of its imperatives where their substance does not present itself as just to those upon whom they are to be imposed.

The theory, it is said, separates law from justice. It does, indeed, separate the one from the other, but only in the same way that we separate them in life. When we say that a law is unjust, we admit that there is no necessary connection between the two; the bridge is made by what the law does, and it becomes just through its recognition as just by those to whom it applies. Law, in short, as made is inherently neutral; its just quality is contributed to it by those who receive it. The business of law being the satisfaction of demand, it must depend for its translation into a moral attribute upon its success in fulfilling its function. And this can only be known as those who meet it report the results of its operation. We cannot, for instance, say that a franchise law is just which confines the right to vote exclusively to men, if women denounce it as unjust.

We cannot argue that the British Trade Union Act of 1927 is just, if trade-unionists widely denounce it as class-legislation. Each of these statutes was law, since it was promulgated by the authority formally competent to legislate upon the subject; but neither of them was justice unless it was recognised as such by those upon whom its consequences were imposed.

Nor need we be impressed by the objection that this view refuses to see in the activities of the state the philosophic purpose for which it stands. Again, this is a matter of fact. Is the life of each citizen so circumstanced that he is able to realise the full potentialities of his nature? Does the state, that is, in fact, secure to him the system of rights without which, as I have argued, that realisation is impossible? There is no other way than this which enables us rightly to decide upon the character of the state. No one could honestly say that the French state before 1789, or the Russian state before 1917, disposed of a body of legal imperatives which sought the well-being of all their subjects, and were regarded by those subjects as embodying that search. If it is replied that the state must be given the credit of good intentions, of a desire to do its best, the answer surely is that this is a matter upon which those who live by the consequences of its acts can alone decide. Frenchmen in 1789, Russians in 1917, clearly decided that the system under which they lived could not secure the satisfaction of demands which, in their judgment, they were entitled to have satisfied. I do not see how it is possible to go behind that decision.

IV

It follows that the legal imperatives of any state must always be conceived, if they are to be capable of justification, in terms of the end it seeks to serve; they are, so to say, a permanent essay in the conditional mood. And if we so regard the state, it follows that its government is a trust, the fulfilment of which must be judged by those who are entitled to expect benefit from its operations.

Now any government, in the last analysis, is a body of men issuing orders to their fellw-citizens in the name of the state. Their retention of power depends upon their ability to issue orders wisely. They are surrounded by innumerable demands, of greater or less intensity, which seek satisfaction from them. The wisdom of their actions, as a government, is clearly dependent upon their ability to maximise the response they make. And to maximise tha· response, the more fully they know the minds and hearts of their subjects, the more likely they are to be able to gauge the policy they should undertake. That is the reason why freedom and equality are important in a society. Freedom alone makes it possible for demands to be formulated; equality provides the only assurance we have that they will be fairly weighed.

Both freedom and equality exist when the system of rights I have described is in active operation in the state. But if a man is a social creature, it is also true that, politically, he is the inert creature of tradition. He is rarely, as an individual, conscious of his power; he is still more rarely able, again as an individual, even when so conscious, to gain attention for his wants. The very size of the modern state makes the individual citizen a voice crying in the wilderness. It is only as he is organised with others of like mind to press his claims, that the demand he makes can hope for effectiveness. Association are therefore of primary importance. They make known the significance of experience to which attention might not, otherwise, be given. They represent the self-created efforts of men to secure a place for themselves in the sun. Not all of them, indeed, are relevant to the purpose of the state; a cricket-club, for example, is usually devoid of any political context. But many associations are dependent for their success upon their ability to translate the result of their effort into the legislation of the state. An employers' federation, a trade-union, a society for the promotion of a national theatre, all seek to make their wills a part of the state-will. The rationale of their existence lies in their effort to change the substance of the legal imperatives of which the state disposes.

Now voluntary associations live by their power to fulfil wants. The state does not give them life; often enough, as with the British trade-unions before 1824, they live in the state's despite. They are the spontaneous expression of felt needs in the experience of men. And since the life of society is too vast to be capable, even if it were desirable, of government by the state alone, no small part of its direction depends upon them. Indeed, it may be argued that, in any society, the richer the variety of group-life, the fuller will be the quality of satisfaction that it obtains. From this, I think, the inference must be drawn that the less the state interferes with the life of associations, the better it will be for both. Its supremacy over them should remain, so far as possible, merely formal and unasserted. It should recognise their inherent right to be; and it should admit that there are aspects of life, the religious, for example, in which an effort on its part to emphasise its superiority can result only in social loss. For where fundamental beliefs are concerned, the command of the state will appear empty and meaningless compared with the appeal that is made to citizens by the association they have voluntarily chosen to express their outlook. In this context, state-sovereignty does not come charged with the requisite emotional penumbra out of which effective and successful allegiance can be made.

It follows from this that any society, at bottom, is essentially federal in nature. The state is, formal law apart, one with other associations, and not over and above them. Its legal imperatives succeed by being in creative relationship with those which other associations lay down for their members. What, in fact, it should largely seek to register as law is the body of demands it encounters among them which represent the largest total of satisfaction in society. And it should not attempt the making of law without an effort effectively to consult those who will be affected by the result of its operations. For successful law is, almost always, that which carries with it, as it is applied, the largest body of experience available for the purposes of administration. Everyone knows, for example, that the success of a great scheme like the Health Insurance system in England was built upon prior consultation, at every point, with medical associations and approved societies. The law worked well because pains were taken, at each point of administration, to convince those who had experience of its subject-matter and were related to the result of its working. Discussion produces, if not consent, at least the impression in those affected that their knowledge has been used, their experience weighed, in the making of decisions. The registering will is that of the state; but the process by which the stage of registration is reached is one which does not leave the citizens concerned with the sense that the state is either above or against them. They have that sense of creativeness which comes from being an active and integral part of the law-making process.

This example, I suggest, points the way to an important truth. Because society is essentially federal, the more the monistic character of law can remain purely formal, the better for society. The more the interest-units which we call associations are integrally related to the process of government, the more effective is likely to be not merely the substance of the law that is to be made, but its operation when it has become law. No government constitutionally chosen can, let us agree, abdicate its right to make its own decisions so long as it is a government; but, also, no government is so likely to remain a government as one which convinces its citizens of the effort it is making to satisfy their demands. And, granted the part played in society by voluntary associations, the best way to produce that conviction is to give them a direct and integral relationship to the process of administration. Men who have not been consulted about a change which affects their lives never feel the same confidence about its rightness, or the same goodwill about its possibilities, as men who feel that, even when their experience has been rejected, a genuine effort has been made to take full account of their attitude. No small part of the failure of modern governments lies in the fact that their institutional system lies over against the interests they have to satisfy instead of seeking to be in and with them as it moves on its way.

This hypothesis, moreover, leads to another principle, the importance of which can hardly be over-emphasised. Because society is federal in its nature, the more widely power is dispersed in a state, the more effective are its operations likely to be. There are three primary reasons why this should be the case. Above all, there is the fact that the more men have responsibility for the result of law, the more likely they are to be interested in its result. Obedience is rarely creative in a highly centralised state. It becomes mechanical and inert, and the sense of responsible co-operation which is always wanted in times of urgency, cannot be found when it is needed. Centralisation, in the second place, makes for uniformity; it lacks the genius of time and place. The scale of its operations makes experiment a difficult matter, for the cost of failure is usually too great to make novelty attractive to an administrator whose first rule is the need for a minimum of error. And centralisation, finally, means an inability to cope with the problem of time in government. Bodies like a cabinet and a legislative assembly can only work so many hours in the day. In a centralised system, they are overwhelmed by the number and variety of issues with which they have to deal. That pressure means that many things demanding consideration are never dealt with at all, and that, only too often, what needs the fullest consideration is only hastily discussed. British political institutions offer, at the moment, a signal example of the dangers of this position. A Parliament which has responsibility for the Colonial Empire can, normally, only find two days a year to discuss its problems; and the Cabinet sees the Budget for the first time only a few hours before it is introduced into the House of Commons.

Now centralisation was less dangerous a hundred years ago than now, simply because the ambit of state-activity was so much smaller. Where, as with ourselves, it reaches long fingers into every nook and cranny of the social fabric, rapid and flexible action is essential. But this, I think, postulates a de-centralised state possessing institutions which are adequately related to the functions with which it deals. The problem is not merely geographical in character. It is, of course, important that London and Manchester, New York, Berlin and Paris, should be fully responsible for, and independent of, the central government in all matters that are local in character; and that they should not, in such matters, have to seek authority from that government in attempting novelty. But, equally, the problem is a functional one. Interest-units, the cotton industry, for example, need their appropriate governmental institutions not less than Lancashire or Kansas or Baden. There is a sphere in which, under appropriate safeguards, they require to make exactly the same order of rules for their governance as Vienna can make for itself, or Liverpool, or Tokyo. To put all legisla-tion upon the territorial plane, or, for the matter of that, all jurisprudence, is to mistake the nature of the interests at work in society. Until we have so related the legal imperatives of the state to the institutions appropriate to their incidence at each period, it is impossible for them to operate successfully. Not a little of the malaise of modern civilisation is due to the fact that the institutions of the state have not kept pace with other changes, particularly economic, in the society it attempts to control.

V

This discussion may perhaps be summarised by saying that our need, in political philosophy, is above all for a theory of the state which attempts the continuous socialisation of the law. The weakness of the modern state lies in the assumptions upon which its legal imperatives are based. It is organised, like every social system, around an idea of justice. But that idea thinks of the individual essentially as the owner of property; and it is for his protection that it is above all concerned. It represents the philosophy of the eighteenth century, the desire of the bourgeosie to safeguard itself against the assault of arbitrary power. But the freedom and equality it secured were, above all, freedom and equality for the owner of property; anyone who examines, from this angle, the Civil Codes of France and Germany, would hardly know, from their basic principles, that there existed vast numbers of men and women who had no property except their labour of which to dispose. It protected in them a freedom of contract which, as against the employer who engaged them, it was simple illusion to suppose them to possess. The need we confront is to extend in fact the privileges offered by our legal imperatives to the whole body of citizens.

Our position, in fact, is not unlike that which the plebs confronted in Rome before it received the protection of its special tribune and the law of the Twelve Tables. Both of these were efforts to make more comprehensive the ambit of an idea of justice. Exactly as, previously, the plebeian who had no gens, had also no law, so, in fact, with ourselves, the citizen who is without property cannot, in any real way, enjoy the rights which are theoretically at his disposal. And because, increasingly he is conscious both of intellectual and economic emancipation, and has forced the state to admit within its categories of recognition, both national education and trade-unions, so he is forcing the state to extend its conception of justice so as to include his interests not less than those of the owners of

property. There are, of course, obstacles in the way. The concessions made to his demands are as partial as those which the
patricians were prepared to make to the plebeians; the system
does not change uniformly upon a single front. Our protection,
for instance, of the individual worker's freedom of contract
outside the standard conditions set by the trade-union is as
much a reservation of privilege to the employer as was secured
by the preponderance of the Roman aristocracy in the legislative assembly at Rome. Tradition and precedent in jurisprudence still operate adversely to the working class, as it did
when the college of Pontiffs set the formulae and procedure of
legal actions as a mystery which, before the time of Flavius,
the plebeian could not hope to penetrate.

What happened in Roman law was the emancipation of the
individual, always, be it said, a fragmentary emancipation,
from a status fixed for him at birth. The same is happening
with ourselves. A new economic order presupposes a change
in the substance of legal imperatives; it forces them to attempt
response to wider demands lest they cease to be legal imperatives. The new economic order means universal suffrage;
universal suffrage means the conquest by the multitude of the
power to operate political institutions. They are bound to use
that power so to operate them as to make them responsive to
needs not so far met by the habits of the state. Their authority
makes things seem a natural part of justice which, even a
generation ago, would have been deemed impracticable by
statesmen. They impose upon society conditions favourable to
their own preponderance in exactly the same way as their pre-
decessors. Law, morality, religion, move in terms of the new
rhythm of life just as they have done when other classes attain
to power. They elevate the conceptions of which they have
need into the same objects of veneration that other conceptions
have had in previous social systems. For a class which dominates
a state does not merely ask for power to exploit those whom it

dispossesses; it demands, as in Soviet Russia to-day, that its exploitation should be equated with right, that its very victims should recognise the justice of the principles upon which they lose their privileges. So, in the past, society regarded an attack on property as the highest sin; and it was prepared to regard as honourable the man who left his wife and children hungry rather than injure the possessions of his neighbour.

What, I have argued, is occurring is an enlargement of the ambit of law. The system of rights I have postulated as inherent in modern social conditions is being transformed from moral claims into positive legal obligations. The property of the individual is deliberately expropriated by the state to this end. The amenities which were dependent upon its ownership are now increasingly organised for the multitude by the state at the cost of those who are able to enjoy them without state-action. And this realisation of rights is a result of a wider conception of justice permeating the social system through a changing emphasis of economic power.

Two final remarks may be made. There is no reason to suppose that the process is an inevitable one; nor can we necessarily count upon its peaceful accomplishment. Of the first, we can only say that the present character of economic evolution implies a transfer of authority to the multitude, and, with that transfer, the emphasis of legal imperatives to its interest instead of to the interest of a small class. But were the economic system suddenly to change in some unexpected direction, those to whom power drifted as a result of that change would certainly alter the substance of rights in their own interest.

We cannot, either, count certainly upon the peaceful accomplishment of change. Men hold fast by their ideas of justice, and it is not often that they abdicate voluntarily from power. Peace seems to be a function of the continuity with which concessions are made to effect a correspondence between legal

authority and political power. Where that correspondence is
unattainable within the framework of a constitution, the new
order imposes its will by force. Such a change may well have
the character of a catastrophe; for modern civilisation is dependent upon mechanisms so complex and so fragile that they
are not likely to survive the use of violence upon any considerable scale. Reason, therefore, suggests a policy of continuous
reform; but man is not wholly a rational animal, and we have no
assurance that reason will be victorious.

CHAPTER THREE

The Organisation of the State

THE problem of the organisation of a state is that of the relationship between its subjects and the law. They may share in its making, in which case, in varying degree, the state is a democracy; or it may be imposed upon them without such participation, in which case, again in varying degree, the state is an autocracy.

Neither type of organisation can exist in a pure form. A complete democracy would consult all of its citizens upon all matters which arose for decision; and a pure autocracy would itself both elaborate and apply the whole system of legal imperatives in the state. With communities of the modern size, it is materially impossible for either type to operate upon this basis.

What we actually encounter in ordinary life is a mixed form of state. In some communities, as in France or Great Britain, the democratic element tends to predominate; in others, as in Russia or Spain, the autocratic element is more obviously emphasised. Every possible combination occurs. A democratic legislation may be flanked by an executive with quasi-autocratic powers. A legislature, itself controlled by the electorate, may, as in Switzerland, almost wholly dominate the executive. Or, as in the United States, the competence of both legislature and executive may be determined by the judiciary, the power of which is, in its turn, subject to constitutional amendment.

The forms of any actual state are determined by its historical traditions; and the nice shades of peculiar emphasis which the experience of a people contributes to their life makes it impossible to insist that any given system of categories is superior to any other. We can argue only that, on general grounds, the democratic form is more suitable than the autocratic, at least to the habits of Western civilisation. For democracy, with all its weaknesses, enables the widest body of demand to be taken into account in shaping the legal imperatives of a state. It makes criticism of their operation the basis of their life. It increases initiative by widening the sense of responsibility. It gives the citizen not merely the sense of sharing in decision, but the actual opportunity to influence its substance. Granted, as experience seems to suggest, that a democratic system is bound to work more slowly than its alternative, simply because the variety of wills it encounters is so much greater, there is no other system which has the same merit of meeting, as an institutional scheme, the theoretical end that the state must serve.

But to say that a state requires democratic form is not to settle the institutions through which that form receives expression; for, broadly speaking, it is not untrue to say that democracy has not, in any certain fashion, discovered its appropriate institutions. Any analysis of a system of legal imperatives seems to disclose the need for three types of authority: (I) We require bodies which lay down general rules applying either to the whole citizen-body, or to such a part of it as possesses a well-defined interest obviously distinct from that of the whole. Such bodies are legislative in character. They may either, as with the King in Parliament, be the supreme legislature, or, as with the City Council of Manchester, be a non-sovereign law-making body the competence of which is fixed by the statute from which its authority derives. (II) We require bodies the duty of which is to carry out the objects of the rules laid down by the legislature under which they work. The essence of such bodies is that they do not, as a general rule, determine their own competence. The principles under which they live are set for them by the legislature to which they are normally answerable. The perspective of their operations must lie within the ambit of the rights laid down by such a legislature. Their business is the execution of the legal imperatives which shape the contours of political life. (III) We require bodies, further, which settle two forms of dispute. There are disputes between the citizen and the executive; the former claims, for example, that some act of the executive goes beyond the competence it possesses. Obviously, if the executive could determine its own competence, it would, in fact, be the master of the legal imperatives by which it lives. By entrusting the decision of such disputes to a body outside the executive, an independent assessment of validity can be obtained. There are, secondly, disputes between citizens. A claims to have been wronged by B. It is necessary to decide whether the conduct of which A complains is in fact prohibited by the legal imperatives of the state; if it is so prohibited, it is necessary also within the terms of the law, to settle upon an appropriate penalty.

At least since the time of Aristotle, it has been the constant postulate of political philosophy that in every well-ordered state these three types of body should be separated from one another both as to the function they perform and the persons who are their members. Some thinkers, Montesquieu for example, have even gone so far as to claim that their separation is the secret of political freedom.

We can hardly accept so rigorous a view. On the ground of pure theory, in the first place, the judicial function can, most logically, be regarded as the province of the legislature; since no body can more appropriately be held to know the meaning of the law than that which makes it. In practice, moreover, it is impossible to maintain any rigorous separation. Legislatures could not properly fulfil their task unless they were able both to interfere in the execution of law, and also, on occasion, to over-

D

rule by statute the decisions of judges the results of which are widely felt to be unsatisfactory. An executive is bound, in applying the law, to clothe general principle in the garment of detail; and, in the modern state, this function covers so wide an ambit that it is often difficult to distinguish it from the work of the legislature. The judiciary, finally, which settles either the competence of the executive (in which case it determines the substance of legislative will) or a dispute between two citizens (in which case it extends the legal imperatives of a state to cover new ground or denies that the ground involved comes within the ambit of those imperatives) is in fact performing a function which is legislative in character. In England and America, for example, what is called, and rightly, judge-made law probably covers an area wider than that of statute; and, in America, the fact that all legislatures are non-sovereign in character, since their authority is derived from written constitutions which they cannot change, gives to the judges who interpret those constitutions, as in cases where the authority either of a statute or an executive is challenged, a power that is greater than that of the legislature itself, since the judicial will is the chief factor in deciding the limits of legislative competence.

Two further principles of a general kind it is necessary to discuss before we turn to the separate analysis of individual institutions. Every well-ordered state possesses a constitution which determines the ultimate way in which its legal imperatives are made. Such constitutions may be divided in two ways. They may be written or unwritten; and they may be flexible or rigid. The Constitution of the United States, for example, is a document which settles the mutual relationships of legislature, executive, and judiciary; and none of these is competent to act save as it can prove the derivation of the power it proposes to take from the clauses of that document. The British Constitution, on the other hand, consists of a mass of statutes, judicial decisions, and unwritten conventions, the real relationship of which is formally determined by the fact that the King in Parliament has the power to alter them as he thinks fit; in technical terms, ordinary legislation and constitutional legislation are on the same footing. The Congress of the United States, for example, is powerless to alter the functions of the president; but the King in Parliament can alter the power of the British executive whenever he thinks fit.

In the modern world, the written constitution is increasingly the general rule; it is felt that the distribution of power in a state is a matter so important that it needs the precision which such an instrument provides. On the whole, experience suggests that there is real weight behind this view; for some constitutional principles are so important that their supremacy cannot be too strongly emphasised. On the other hand, it is highly undesirable that any constitution should be rigid in character. The needs of a community change, and the formal structure it requires changes with an alteration of those needs. The rigidity of the American Constitution, for example, is notorious; it can be changed only by a resolution of two-thirds of each House of Congress, assented to, in a period of seven years, by three-fourths of the constituent states of the American federation. Experience has shown that to make the power to amend a process so difficult to operate means a failure to secure necessary adjustments when they become clearly desirable. The original distribution of powers in the United States makes it almost impossible, for example, to secure that uniformity in labo r legislation and marital arrangements which are essential in the modern world. In a backward state of the federation, the reactionary employer is unduly advantaged; and the 'full faith and credit' clause of the Constitution involves, in practice, divorce facilities for the rich which are not at the disposal of the poor. The conclusion of experience seems to be the desirability of a written constitution which can be amended by a direct and simple process. On the whole, it is probable that the best method is to require the legislature to amend the Constitution, but to insist that a specially high proportion of the members shall support any change that is proposed.

It is sometimes argued that a democratic system requires the embodiment of the initiative and the referendum in the constitution. A people, it is said, does not really control its own life if its only direct participation in the business of making legal imperatives is confined to choosing the persons responsible for their substance. By the initiative, the popular will can take positive form; and by the referendum, the people can prevent action by its representatives with which it is not in agreement. Direct government, it is claimed, provides a necessary supplement to a representative system; otherwise, as Rousseau said of the English people, it is free only at election-time.

But this is, it may be suggested, both to mistake the nature of the problems which have to be decided, and the place at which popular opinion can obtain the most valuable results in action. In all modern states, the size of the electorate is necessarily so large that the people can hardly do more, as a whole people, than give a direct negative or affirmative to the questions direct government would place before them. Legislation, however, is a matter not less of detail than of principle; and no electorate can deal with the details of a measure submitted to it for consideration. Direct government, in fact, is too crude an instrument for the purposes of modern government. It fails to make discussion effective at the point where discussion is required; and it leaves no room for the process of amendment. One might, it is true, leave certain broad questions of principle to popular vote, whether, for instance, the supply of electricity should be a national or a private service. But all other questions are so delicate and complex that the electorate would have neither the interest nor the knowledge, when taken as an undifferentiated electorate, to arrive at adequate decisions.

Nor is this all. Not only can most questions not be framed in a way which can make direct government effective; the secondary results of the system are also unsatisfactory. It is hardly compatible, for instance, with the parliamentary system since it places the essential responsibility for measures outside the legislature. Such a division of responsibility destroys that coherence of effort which enables a people adequately to judge the work of its representatives. It assumes, further, that public opinion exists about the process of legislation, as well as about its results. But the real problem of government is not forcibly to extract from the electorate an undifferentiated and uninterested opinion upon measures about which it is unlikely to be closely informed. It is rather to relate to the law-making process that part of public opinion which is relevant to, and competent about, its substance before that substance is made a legal imperative. This involves not direct government, but a method of associating the relevant interest-units of the community with the making of the measures which will affect their lives. A referendum, for example, on a national scheme of health insurance would give far less valuable results than a technique of consultation in which the opinions of doctors, trade-unions, and similar associations were given a full opportunity to state their views before the scheme was debated in the legislative assembly. Effective opinion for the purpose of government, in a word, is almost always opinion which is organised and differentiated from that of the multitude by the possession of special knowledge. Popular opinion, as such, will rarely give other than negative results; and it seems to be the lesson of experience, very notably on the record of Switzerland, that it is so firmly encased in traditional habit, as to make social experiment difficult when it is a reserve-power-outside.

II

The legislature of a state needs, under modern conditions, to be based on universal suffrage if it is to speak with proper authority to its constituents. It must be large enough to enable its members to keep in effective touch with the electorate, and small enough to enable genuine discussion to take place; in a body, for instance, as large as the Congress of the Russian Soviet Government all individuality in debate is lost, and the assembly becomes a mere organ of registration for the will of the dominant party-machine. It must submit itself for re-election to the citizens at the end of a given term the length of which it is itself unable, under normal conditions, to alter. This term must be long enough to secure two results: The legislature must be able to make itself responsible for an ample programme, and its members must have time enough thoroughly to acquaint themselves with the operation of its procedure. But the term, also, must be short enough to make it certain that the legislature does not lose touch with its constituents. The system which obtained in England, before 1911, of a seven-year period between elections was too long because it gave the legislature a life too little affected by the flow of public opinion; on the other hand, the two-year period of the House of Representatives in the United States is too short, because as soon as the member has been elected, his re-election begins to dominate his mind, and he can rarely hope to learn, in so short a period, his way about its legislative methods. On the whole, it appears that a life of about five years corresponds to these requirements.

Normally, a member of the legislative assembly will be elected to it as the supporter of a party. In the modern state, the electorate is so large, the number of interests so varied, that it is necessary to organise them for the purpose of arriving at decisions. This is the function which parties perform in the state; they act as the brokers of ideas. They choose the principles which they think most likely to secure acceptance from the electorate and take their stand upon those principles which they promise, so far as possible, to translate into legislation. Broadly speaking, the party-system is the necessary basis of representative government. Without it, we could not secure either a coherent programme of measures, nor the necessary volume of organised support for them in the legislative assembly to enable them to reach the statute-book. With all their defects, they represent the articulate expression of a way of life which has grown out of effective civic demand.

The division of parties does not, of course, directly correspond to the division of opinion among members of the state. Upon this absence of correspondence, two principles are often founded, both of which are attractive in their assumptions, and unsatisfactory in their operation. Where party-government dominates the life of a state, it is clear that the method of dividing opinion is highly artificial; in England, for example, if only the Conservative Party and the Labour Party existed, many citizens would have to choose between alternatives with neither of which were they in full and creative sympathy. It is therefore urged that a multiple party-system, usually termed the group-system, more effectively corresponds to the division of public opinion.

But, on the experience of the group-system, as in France and Weimar Germany, it seems to be attended with two fatal defects. The most important of these is the fact that, where it operates, the only way to control a legislature is to organise such a coalition of groups as will produce a majority capable of dominating the legislature; and the result of this is to substitute manœuvre for responsibility and to make policy devoid of that coherence and amplitude which enables it to be effectively judged. The second defect, which is seen very notably in France, is that the group-system tends to aggregate power around persons rather than about principles. The average voter can discriminate in France between, for instance, the royalist and the socialist groups; but in between them is a large number the differences between which are hardly capable of effective statement. The result is that whereas in Great Britain and the United States, the voter knows clearly the kind of result he is seeking to obtain, and can assume that a victory for his party will mean the kind of legislation that result implies, in France, so long as the extremes of right and left are not in office, there is no relationship, of any direct kind, between the expressed will of the electorate and the kind of government under which it will live. It is, moreover, a further defect that the defeat of the government in the legislative assembly depends less upon disagreement about principle, than upon a struggle between the different groups for that particular coalition which will maximise for each party to it the enjoyment of the spoils of power.

This absence of correspondence, secondly, leads to the insistence that membership of the legislative assembly should be determined by proportional representation. The strength of parties, it is said, should correspond there to the volume of support each obtains from the electorate; on any other system of choice, the expressed will of the electors is thwarted, and the resultant legislation may even be the negation of public opinion. A system which, like that of Great Britain, simply divides the territory of the state into a number of broadly equal constituencies and awards the seat to the candidate who has the largest number of votes, may have the vicious effect of giving one party a number of seats entirely out of proportion to the total support it has obtained in the whole territory, and may have the further disadvantage of leaving large blocks of public opinion without any representation at all proportionate to their strength. In the general election of 1924, for example, the Conservative Party had a large majority in the House of Commons, but was in a considerable minority of total votes; while the Liberal Party, which still polls millions of votes, obtains only a small number of seats in derisory proportion to the actual supporters it can claim.

It is clear that there is real substance in the criticism. But we must consider not only the theoretical merits of proportional representation, but also its actual working. Wherever it operates, it has had two outstanding results: (I) it always increases the power of party-machines; (II) it so balances the strength of parties in the legislative assembly that it often produces minority-government, which makes coherent legislation impossible, or compels coalition government which, as it works, has all the vices of the group-system. In actual practice, moreover, the single-member system sets limits to what a government can do with its majority, where this has been unfairly obtained, which it is difficult not to respect. In England in 1924, for example, the Conservative Government had the power, if it wished, to attempt both the reform of the House of Lords and the creation of a protective tariff, both of which were ardently desired by its supporters. It could not, in fact, make either effort, because the nature of its majority deprived it of sufficient spiritual strength to do so, and it feared the result of such an attempt at the next general election. It must be remembered, further, that the power of any section of opinion is not measured only by the number of votes it can poll at a general election. In the actual process of law-making the factors which constitute its authority are both more numerous and more subtle than the critics of the present system are prepared to recognise. It is worth while, too, to insist that any government which goes beyond the implicit limits of its actual authority, which uses, that is, its majority unfairly, is pretty certain not only to pay the penalty at the subsequent general election, but also to have its measures amended by the government which succeeds it in office.

Any limitations upon the right to membership of the legis-lative assembly ought to bear equally upon the whole citizen-body, and they should, in general, be as few as possible. But it is not improbable that we should demand more rigorous tests of adequacy than we do. At present, once the test of age has been satisfied, practically no other criterion is required. This means in practice, that wealth, birth, relevance to a powerful voluntary body (the National Union of Mineworkers, for example) or membership of a profession which, like that of the law, is peculiarly adapted to membership of a legislative assembly, have special opportunities hardly open to other citizens. It may, I think, be reasonably argued that anyone who desires membership should offer proof of experience in the kind of work a legislative assembly performs. If, for example, we demanded as a prerequisite of election, that every candidate should have served for a term of years on such a body as a municipal council, or its equivalent, it is not improbable that we should greatly improve the quality of members. It is important, also, that members should be paid. Otherwise poor men can hardly hope to get elected at all; and none save the rich will be able to devote their whole time to legislative work.

A legislative assembly should, in general, consist of a single chamber. Wherever, in any unitary state, a bicameral system exists, it will be found on examination that it tends to secure, as with the House of Lords in England, the predominance of some special interest in the state. On theory, indeed, it is difficult to see any case for a second chamber; as Siéyès said, if it agrees with the first, it is superfluous, and if it disagrees, it is obnoxious. The domination of special interests apart, the case for a second chamber is usually made on two grounds. It is necessary, it is argued, to prevent ill-considered and precipitate legislation by the first chamber; and it is important to have a body capable of giving the requisite technical revision to the measures which the government proposes. But this is to raise questions (a) of the composition and (b) of the functions and competence of the second chamber. Parenthetically, it may be observed that, even in a federal state, the two-chamber system has always resulted in one or other of the two chambers, as with the Senate of the United States, obtaining an emphatic predominance.

Let us take composition first. A purely nominated second chamber, the House of Lords, for example, or the Canadian Senate, cannot possibly have the authority, at least in a democratic state, to challenge the will of an elected assembly; and its membership will depend, whenever vacancies occur, simply on the will of those who at that moment have the right to nominate. An elected second chamber is hardly in better case. If it is chosen at the same time, and upon the same franchise, as the first, it will merely reflect its composition; if at a different time, still more upon a different franchise, it will probably hamper the work of the government in power, and, to the degree that its franchise is limited, be excessively weighted as with the French Senate, to protect the interests that limited franchise emphasises. It has been suggested that neither nomination nor election upon a territorial basis is satisfactory, and that the basis of a second chamber should be occupational interests. But no method is known of giving proper proportional weight to occupational interests; and if, for instance, the engineering profession sent one of its members to such a body, his views, as an engineer, would be totally devoid of relevance to the vast majority of the decisions it had to take. To attain coherence, in a word, an occupational second chamber would have to elect its members upon a party-basis, and this would destroy the very purpose which occupational representation was intended to serve.

Nor are functions and competence easier problems to resolve. It is difficult to treat seriously the argument that a chamber with the power to delay is necessary. For, in the first place, no government attempts any large-scale legislation until its substance has become a commonplace of discussion; and, in the second, if the delay is at all long, the work of the primary chamber is largely wasted. Anyone who bears in mind the time it has taken in Great Britain to bring great measures like electoral reform, Irish Home Rule, or national education to the statute-book, will be tempted to demand a technique for hastening the passage of legislation, rather than for delaying it. Nor is there substance in the view that a second chamber is needed to perform the work of technical revision. This is, in its nature, drafting work, which requires the services not of a chamber, but of a small number of specialists in that art. On the problem of competence, this only need be said, that no second chamber could have the authority of the first unless it was similarly elected; and to give it lesser authority is to raise at once the problem of composition, which, I have argued, is incapable of satisfactory solution, and of the right of the first chamber to make its will prevail.

A word is necessary about the position of a second chamber in a federal state. This is held to be necessary on two grounds: (I) the constituent units of the federation must be represented, and (II) the distribution of powers which the constitution organises must be protected from invasion. But the first argument is surely superfluous, since the constituent units already control, by their own governments, the matters entrusted to them by the constitution; and such protection of the distribution of powers as is necessary can be obtained without a second chamber by making the amendment of the constitution dependent upon a large measure of assent from the totality of units whose competence is to be altered. On the experience of the American Senate—the classic institution of this kind—I do not think it could seriously be argued that its results show any special value as a safeguard against excessive centralism; and the experience of Australia seems to indicate the danger of a system which, by emphasising an artificial equality where none exists, prevents necessary change from being made at the proper time.

Into the details of legislative organisation I cannot here enter.

All I can do is to indicate certain general principles which experience seems to have definitely established. The classical British system, in which the political executive, as a committee of the dominant party in the legislative assembly, is an inherent part of that body, and directs its work, is clearly preferable to the American system (itself largely an historical accident) which separates them. Such fusion makes not only for coherent planning, but also for obvious responsibility; and it enables the legislature to be used, as it ought to be used, as the chief means of selecting men who are suitable for posts of executive responsibility. It is important, secondly, to differentiate in legislative work, between discussion of principle and discussion of detail. The first belongs naturally to the legislature as a whole; the second is best entrusted to small committees of its members less on the model of the British House of Commons, than of that developed by such subordinate assemblies in England as the London County Council. This implies, also, the desirability of a close association between the legislative assembly and the process of administration. For this purpose, each department of state should be flanked by an advisory committee of members of the legislative assembly with the right to be consulted upon legislative projects to report upon the working of delegated legislation, and to investigate such problems within the Department as seem to call for enquiry. It is important to retain the responsibility of the minister for the policy of his department; but the necessity for a closer connection between his work and that of the legislature has been made obvious by experience. Otherwise, as a general rule, the assembly, subject to occasional revolts, becomes a mere organ of registration for the dictates of the executive.

I have suggested that some such term as five years is the proper length of life for a legislature. But it is undesirable that this should be, as in the United States, a fixed term. Occasions arise when it is desirable to consult the people, as when a new and vital issue comes suddenly into view. For such a purpose, or, when a government has been defeated and believes that the legislature is out of touch with public opinion, the power to dissolve is important. Where should that power reside? I see no effective alternative to its residence in the cabinet. That body is the necessary motive power of legislation; its policies are the main subject of debate. Were it to reside in the formal chief of the state, its exercise would involve grave problems about his neutrality; and no legislature could be expected to vote wisely about its own dissolution. It is not a power likely to be abused. For its unwise exercise will not only be visited with the disapproval of the electorate, but those who fail to exercise it wisely are certain, in the long run, to be deposed from control by their own party supporters. The power to dissolve suddenly has the additional merit of enabling the executive to keep its supporters (and opponents) up to the mark, while its dramatic quality maintains a constant interest among the electorate in the proceedings of a legislature. From this angle, it is worth noting that a legislature seems to work at its best when the government majority is large enough to enable it to carry out an ample programme, but not so large as to give it an excessive authority. Popular interest in politics is never so keen as when the government of a state lives in the shadow of possible defeat.

I have already explained that the scale of the modern state requires a large measure of decentralisation if it is to do its work in a creative way. While it is clear that the legislature must remain the formal place in which the legal imperatives of the state are defined, it cannot hope to work well unless a considerable part of its powers are delegated to subordinate bodies. This can best be accomplished in three ways: (I) All matters the perspective of which is geographical in character, for example, local transport, should be devolved upon local elected assemblies, controlling suitable areas. These should have not limited powers, but the right to deal with all matters not specifically determined to be outside their competence. They should have, also, the right to combine for common purposes. The central government should in certain matters, for example education and public health, retain a connection with them by means of grants in aid and the authority to inspect. (II) Within the framework of a general minimum set of conditions determined by the central legislature, there should be devised for industries a system of subordinate legislatures with rule-making powers which, under suitable safeguards, can be compulsorily applied. We should seek, that is, to develop, *mutatis mutandis*, the kind of self-government for industry which has been characteristic of professions like the bar and medicine. (III) There should be devolved upon subordinate bodies, of which the Interstate Commerce Commission in the United States, and the Electricity Authority in Great Britain are good examples, wide rule-making powers in subjects of a technical nature which are not (*a*) easily susceptible to legislative discussion and (*b*) not confined, in the operation of their results, to an obvious and well-defined constituency. In the nature of things, in all three cases, a power of review must be inherent in the central legislature, but it is a general rule that the more it can be kept both minimal and formal, the better is likely to be the quality of administration.

III

The executive of a state has two aspects—the political and the departmental. On the one hand, it is a small body of statesmen who recommend a policy for the acceptance of a legislature and, after its acceptance, are responsible for its application; on the other it is a much larger body of officials who carry out the determinations at which the statesmen have arrived. Obviously, the two categories are more distinct as to persons than as to power: for an important official of long experience, while he is technically the subordinate of his political chief, will have great weight with the latter, and count for much in the making of decisions.

The political heads of a state are usually termed the cabinet. It is advisable and, indeed, essential to good government, that they should be members of the legislative assembly. It is thence that they derive their power, and it is there that they must answer for its exercise. This means that, as a normal rule, the cabinet must be composed of members of the same party, for this alone is likely to give that unity of outlook which makes coherency of policy possible. A cabinet needs to be small; once it passes some such number as a dozen, experience shows that it ceases to possess an inner coherence. Most of its members must be responsible for some great function of administration, foreign policy, finance, trade and commerce. But it requires also a directing and co-ordinating mind, who has no special responsibility for a given department; and at least one other member (who is usually termed a minister without portfolio) whose services can be utilised at any special point of pressure.

The head of the cabinet may either be, as in the United States, also the formal head of the state, or, as in England and France, the offices may be distinct and the chief of the state may be largely a ceremonial personage whose political function is to secure continuity of administration. There is no inherent superiority in either system, though the Anglo-French method is more convenient since it makes it easier for the head of the cabinet to take part, as Prime Minister, in the legislative assembly. He is usually the leader of the party which has attained predominance in that body. How are his colleagues to be chosen? In most states, he himself chooses them from amongst those who will, as he thinks, form, collectively, the most efficient instrument of government; in Australia, on the other hand, the Labour Party chooses its cabinet by means of the party caucus.

There is not, I think, much room for doubt that a Prime Minister ought to be left to choose his own colleagues. The qualities that are required for the direction of a government department are not those which easily lend themselves to assessment by election. The problems of colleagueship and teamwork that are involved imply a technique of discriminating choice for which the process of voting is too crude an instrument. Granted that a Prime Minister will not only make mistakes, but also emphasise unduly the personal equation, he is yet less likely to make mistakes than a body like the Australian Labour Party, or the American people when it chooses a president; the latter system is too like a lottery, and as Bagehot said, success in a lottery is no argument for the method. And the factors which limit the Prime Minister's choice are, generally speaking, a sufficient safeguard. Every party contains men of hardly less standing and stature than himself. He is bound to choose them, and their support will be conditioned by the wisdom of the other nominations he makes. Upon the assumption that they have passed through the rigorous apprenticeship of the legislative assembly, most of those who are chosen for cabinet office are likely to be the obvious nominees for the places they attain.

The non-political side of the executive government raises problems of a different order. Broadly speaking, it raises three types of issue: (I) How is it to be composed and organised? (II) What are its functions? (III) What are to be its relations to the public it ultimately serves? Obviously, the first and third of these questions is set by our answer to the second. The officials of a state carry out the orders of their political chiefs. The business of ministers is to frame a policy which satisfies the largest possible volume of public demand and, on its acceptance by the legislature, to maximise its effective operation. Obviously, also, in the scale of the modern state, they can give no more than a general oversight to this task. They must be dependent upon their officials for knowledge of public demand, for information in detail upon the possible ways of responding to it, and for the daily and detailed work of carrying out the law. No matter what the complexion of the party in power, these tasks must be performed with a minimum of friction.

To this end, officials need to be neutral; they must serve one party in power as wholeheartedly and as efficiently as another. To be neutral, they must be assured, granted their competence, permanence of tenure; and to give them encouragement to do their best, the system of promotion must give to ability the largest possible chance of being discovered and exercising a proportionate responsibility. To secure these qualities, the appointment of officials should always be in the hands of a commission independent of the government of the day; the less pressure that government can exert upon it, the better for the state. In general, the method of choosing officials which the commission should adopt should be one which reduces favouritism to minimal proportions; and, broadly speaking, competitive examination is, for all except technical posts, the best means to this end. Once a candidate has been admitted to the service, granted competence and good behaviour, he should be certain of keeping his place until the age of retirement. This must be fixed at a sufficiently early age as to secure permanent heads of departments who are in touch with the new ideas of their generation.

It is important, also, that the categories of the official world should be as elastic as possible. The danger of any civil service is bureaucracy, and the highroad thereto is through rigidity of routine and promotion by seniority. To mistake routine for efficiency and antiquity for experience are always the dangers which beset a body of officials. They become afraid of initiative and experiment, and they tend to think that immunity from attack is the proof of a well-ordered department. The first need of a civil service is safeguards against these dangers. There are, indeed, no clear rules for their prevention. Much depends upon the wisdom of the political chiefs; even more, perhaps, on the *esprit de corps* of the service itself. But the main rule is that officials should do their work in the atmosphere of a critical and competent public opinion.

For as it is the public that officials have to serve, so by the public they must be judged. If both service and judgment are to be properly performed, public opinion must be rightly related to the process of administration. To secure this end, the device of the advisory committee is of the first importance. Wherever a department touches a social interest, the associations which serve that interest ought to be related to the department for the purpose of consultative co-operation. A department of education, for instance, ought at each step of its work, to be in continuous touch with organised bodies of teachers, doctors, psychologists, parents. Without adequate mechanisms for this end, the work of administration will lack not only creativeness, but also that pungent sensitiveness to its results which is the real test of its quality. No better means exist than the advisory committee for the reciprocal training of civil servants and the public. The first learn the art of government by persuasion; the second discovers the point at which reality of claim is distorted by their natural offspring of passion and propaganda. No small part of the prospect of constitutional government depends upon the wisdom with which it exploits this instrument.

Certain consequences of neutrality in officials, and of their position as servants of the state, need, in conclusion, a brief explanation. If both the government and the general community are to have confidence in that neutrality, it follows, I think, that all civil servants who take part in the making of policy must refrain from taking part in political life. That exclusion need not apply to minor officials; but no minister, say of a conservative complexion, would easily feel confidence in his permanent secretary if he knew that the latter devoted his evenings to ardent socialist propaganda. The same restriction seems logically to apply to political candidates; a high official cannot expect to enter a legislative assembly, and, on defeat, return to the civil service. What has been said here of officials applies with even greater pertinence to the armed forces of the state and to the police. The cultivation in them of political habits would be fatal to that unquestioning acceptance of civilian orders upon which, under ordinary conditions, the well-being of the state depends. Bias at as pivotal a point is bound, sooner or later, to make officials a Praetorian guard; and the step therefrom to autocracy is as inevitable as it is short.

This raises, of course, the question of the limits of freedom of association among state officials. The problem is complicated; and I can here only state certain conclusions in dogmatic form. The relation of the armed forces and the police to the state make it necessary legally to prohibit their right to strike; but they are entitled, in compensation, to the full development of that form of self-government which gives to each section of them a full share in the determination of the conditions of their work, and entitles them, where difference arises between them and the government to such an independent arbitration of the issue as is performed in England by a body like the Industrial Court. To civilians, I do not think such a prohibition could either apply or be made effective if it became necessary to attempt its operation. The state, indeed, is entitled to create machinery which insists upon mediating disputes between the government and its servants before they strike; and it is fairly probable that such machinery will usually be successful. But I do not think the state is entitled, as an employer, to insist upon its sovereign character. Its business there, like that of any other employer, is to win the loyalty of its servants by persuading them that its standards are just; and they are entitled to all the normal methods a trade-union takes to improve the

conditions under which they labour. Nor can I see any reason
why the minor officials of a state are not equally entitled to
join with similarly placed workers in outside industry to improve
their conditions by methods that they deem suitable. The glory
of working in a government office is no effective compensation
to clerks or postmen who feel themselves unfairly treated.

IV

I have already explained why the independence of the judiciary
is an important principle in the operation of government. To
this end, three principles are important. (I) The method of
appointment must minimise the possibility of political considerations in the choice of judges; (II) the persons appointed
must, subject to good behaviour, have permanent security of
tenure; (III) promotion must take account of legal eminence
only. The first principle rules out election by either the people
or the legislature as a method of choice; the qualities required
for judicial office cannot be fairly weighed by the criteria which
are suited to an electoral process. There then seem to remain
three possible methods. The judiciary might be, as in France,
a body chosen in the first place by competitive examination,
promotion to higher posts being dependent upon proofs of
ability. There is much to be said for this method; certainly it
has given France a learned body of judges, characterised, at
their best, by a high sense of professional honour. My doubt
of the method is, first, that the qualities required of a judge
include those which the method of admission cannot test; and
compared with the English judge, the Frenchman remains
somewhat narrowly legal in outlook. He is, as a rule, a good
judge; but the narrow discipline within which his life is passed
tends to separate him unduly from non-judicial experience.
A second method is that of England, and for federal appointments, the United States, where the judges are chosen by
executive nomination, both in the lower courts, and in the

higher. The system, undoubtedly, as names like Mansfield and Marshall, Jessel and Bowen and Holmes, show clearly, has given us many great judges; but no one who scrutinises the appointments of the last hundred years can doubt that political considerations play far too large a part in determining its character. I should prefer a third method in which the judges themselves presented the executive with a short list of names outside of which it would go only in the most exceptional circumstances. Similarly, judges should make their own recommendations for promotion, subject only to the limitation that no judge who had only been five years on the bench, or who was within five years of retirement should be eligible for nomination. It is important, I think also, to debar the judiciary from access to political office; and no person who has held political office should be eligible for judicial appointment until three years have elapsed from his retirement. It is, I think, further important to retire judges compulsorily at seventy years of age, with an option of voluntary retirement after fifteen years' service on the bench.

The virtues of such a system are clear. They safeguard us against the danger of a judiciary which has been, from early manhood, shut off from the rest of the world through membership of a narrow, professional caste. They minimise the extent to which a lawyer can secure either promotion or appointment in return for political services. By making the judiciary select, in the first instance, names for executive consideration, they emphasise the right of those with the best experience of professional qualifications to judge the weight which should attach to them; while the exceptional right of the executive to make an alternative choice limits the danger of judicial favouritism. It should be added that I assume the undesirability of a system in which, as in England, the layman can be made a minor judicial official, usually, be it added, as a reward for the lesser political services; the proper place for a layman is on a jury, above all, in criminal cases. Even the ordinary jury is of dubious value in cases where the facts to be judged are of a highly expert character, as, for instance in commercial cases concerning matters like bills of exchange. In this realm, where a jury-system is retained, it is better to have a special panel of persons whose peculiar experience gives their judgment upon the matters involved a special weight.

In any well-ordered state, the working of the law will be characterised by four principles. The torts of government will involve precisely the same responsibility as those of the ordinary citizen; no state can be truly under the rule of law where the acts of its agents do not imply liability of their principal for fault. Sovereignty ought not to procure irresponsibility for those who act in its name. Where, moreover, the executive is entrusted with powers of delegated legislation, the question of the legal limit of those powers ought always to be decided by the ordinary courts. It is essential, thirdly, that judicial procedure should never be so costly as to deprive the poor citizen of access to the courts; it is even better to have a large number of frivolous actions than to leave men in the belief that their lack of means prevents them from seeking to attain justice. The reform, finally, of legal methods must be the constant preoccupation of the state. To this end, it is necessary not only that there should be continuous enquiry, especially on the criminal side, into the working of judicial institutions; it is important that experience of their operations should be recorded by all who participate in them. A permanent commission on law reform, in which judges, lawyers and laymen alike participate, is one of the most urgent needs of the time.

V

I have spoken constantly here of the importance of public opinion; and it is impossible to conclude this part of the discussion without a reference, however brief, to certain problems which are of its essences. Two things are clear: the quality of public opinion depends upon the truth of the information upon which it is based, and its power to make an impression is a function of the degree to which it is organised. Or, rather, the second principle may perhaps be put best by saying that there is rarely such a thing as a general public opinion. What occurs is rather the development of a series of public opinions centring about the issues which arise; and the relative power of these opinions depends upon the knowledge and organisation they can command.

Now anyone who examines the problem of truth in information in modern society will be struck, first, by its complexity, and, second, by the fact that its collection and dissemination is not an effort at the objective presentation of facts. News becomes propaganda as soon as its substance can affect policy; and, in an unequal society, the incidence of news is tilted to the advantage of the holders of economic power. Most men have to depend for their information upon newspapers. These depend for their support on the advertisements they can command; and their production is so costly that, in general, only the wealthy can afford to establish them. But because they are dependent upon the advertiser, they must, for the most part, print such news and comment as will satisfy those who purchase the commodities the advertiser seeks to sell; otherwise they cannot obtain the circulation among those whose power of effective demand is considerable. The result is a consistent bias in the reporting of news the true incidence of which might embarrass the wealthy classes. Events like the Russian Revolution, a great strike, the operation of a nationalised industry, are distorted so as to produce an unfavourable impression of their nature upon the citizen who learns of their character from his newspaper. He gets his facts as through a mirror in which their perspective is out of proportion to suit a special interest. So long as the interest of men in the result of policy is unequal, the facts to which they have access are selected and weighed to prevent the emergence of their true meaning. It is only in an equal society that it pays to print the truth.

Any public opinion, finally, is strong to the degree that it is organised; and organisation is largely a function of economic power. It is much easier to organise a small body of rich mine-owners, than a large body of poor trade-unionists. It is much easier, also, to maintain the former coherent and united. The impact of error is felt less keenly; the consequences of success are far more direct. Economic power can command knowledge out of all proportion to its own intelligence. It can afford to wait, and it does not find that the contours of its normal life are greatly altered by the need of waiting. But the organisation of men who lack economic power has few of these advantages. Its main weapons are often so costly, as in a strike, that it cannot afford to use them. Its power to purchase knowledge is less, not least because the psychological background of those who possess the knowledge it requires too often makes its bias alien from what such organisation requires. Public opinion in an unequal society, in a word, cannot make its claims in terms of its moral character. Their justice is always limited by the distortion of interest which unequal power impels. No social order, therefore, will ever satisfy the demands of its citizens equally, or ever seriously attempt the equal recognition of their rights, so long as there are serious inequalities in the distribution of economic power.

CHAPTER FOUR

The State and the International Community

I

So far I have discussed the problems of the state as though these concerned only relations with its own citizens. But, in fact, each state in the modern world is only a one among many; and perhaps the most important issues we confront are the problems of external relationships which arise when one state and its citizens have relations with other states and their members. From the postulates already laid down, no state can give orders to another state, for, were that the case, the legal imperatives of the latter would cease to have the character upon which, as we have seen, the internal character of statehood depends.

It is necessary, moreover, to regulate the relationships between states; international law is a body of rules by which the mutual contacts of states and their citizens are organised. They are imposed upon men living in society by the fact that, without them, once we move from the internal to the external characteristics of statehood, we should be presented with a condition for which anarchy would be the only word. If international law is not binding upon states, then there can be no rules as between them except the will upon which they determine to act. And, indeed, there have been great thinkers, Hobbes, for example, who have not hesitated to accept this conclusion. They have argued, from their premises quite logically, that the fact that no association of men is entitled to give orders to the state makes it impossible to regard international law as valid in the same way as national law. If, they say, the legal imperatives of the state are to be supreme, no other imperatives can be, logically, superior to them. It then follows that international law is only valid for a given state to the degree that it is prepared to accept its substance. International law, that is, becomes truly law through its recognition as such by definite states. In itself it has no binding force; what gives it authority is its adoption, rule by rule, as a legal imperative by individual states.

But before we accept so drastic a conclusion, it is important to examine its foundations. From this angle, certain significant facts emerge. (I) A new state, when it comes into existence, cannot pick and choose among the settled rules of international law. It finds them binding upon itself exactly as though it were responsible for their creation. International customs, treaties, and arbitration agreements have, in fact, given rise to a body of well-settled principles which, in the normal intercourse of states, limit their activities in the same way, as say, the law of England limits the activities of its citizens. (II) The sovereignty of the state is an historical condition which arises from the breakdown of the medieval *respublica christiana* of the Middle Ages. Broadly speaking, before the Reformation, the will of the state lacked any sovereign character. It was regarded as inherently limited by the law of God and the law of nature; any enactment of the state contrary to their principles was inherently void of effect. We are now witnessing what may be termed a reconstruction of the world-commonwealth of which medieval thinkers dreamed. We have found that scientific and economic change has made it impossible to leave the individual state free to make its own decisions in matters of common world-concern. At decisive points, such unfettered discretion leads to war; and for the same reason that the will of the state secured primacy over all other associations within its territory, so, within the society of states, a common will, with primacy over the will of any given state, has become a political necessity. It follows, therefore that the will of the state must be subject to an overriding will in matters of common world-concern, exactly as the individual will is subject to the system of legal imperatives laid down by the state.

This may, perhaps, best be put in another way. Between 1500 and 1700 the modern state emerged as sovereign because in no other fashion could the lives of its citizens be guaranteed peace and security. To the thinkers who sought a philosophy of its activities what was outstanding in its life was the fact that it had shaken its will free from all external control. They therefore naturally assumed that it was the ultimate unit of social organisation. But conditions, particularly in the last half-century, have changed again. The world has become so inter-dependent that an unfettered will in any state is fatal to the peace of other states. If we leave, say England, free to settle her own frontiers and armaments, her own tariffs and labour standards, the rights she will grant to foreigners in her courts, the method by which she will determine disputes with other states, and so forth, the inevitable result is international disaster. The interdependence of states makes it necessary to postulate a world-community, a society of states, with its own legal imperatives as the ultimate rules before which all other rules must give way. Our conditions, in short, make the postulate of cosmopolitan law-making for matters of common concern as clearly essential as is the legal predominance of the state within its own territory. Municipal law, in a word, should be legally subordinate to international law.

It is possible, therefore, to construct a theory of law upon the hypothesis that its ultimate source is the will of the society of states, and that this will is primary over all other wills in modern civilisation. On such a hypothesis, the relation of a given state to the society of states is one of subordination: it resembles that of, say, New York to the United States of America. There are subjects of legislation upon which New York can make up its own mind; there are other subjects upon which it must accept the decision of the United States. In this view, the state ceases to be sovereign. It must accept the logic of the world-conditions in which it is involved. A demand on its part for unfettered discretion is as impossible of acceptance as a demand by the individual citizen for the legal right to an unlimited will. Common needs imply mutual subordination, and where there is mutual subordination there is not, in the historic and technical sense, the possibility of a sovereign state.

Nor is this view vitiated by the undoubted facts (a) that states break international law and (b) that the society of states has not yet evolved satisfactory organs, especially in the legislative sphere, for the development of international law. An infraction of international law by an individual state is as important, or as insignificant, as an infraction of municipal law by a given individual citizen; the law remains law so long as it is normally and habitually capable of enforcement. We may grant that the institutions of the society of states are as yet inadequate for their purpose. There are two adequate reasons for this. The recognition, in the first place, of international interdependence is comparatively new; in any systematic fashion it can hardly be dated earlier than the Treaty of Versailles in 1919. And, in the second, every attempt to translate this interdependence into institutional terms is met by the ghost of the sovereign state still seeking feverishly to retain in its hands the ruins of its empire. The history of the League of Nations and the United Nations is the record of nothing so much as of a conflict between the new principle of international interdependence and its consequences, and the old principle of sovereignty. The desire to pay service to the latter is seen in the retention of the rule of unanimity by the League for making decisions, and more strikingly in the unanimity rule among the Great Powers in the Security Council of the United Nations. The necessity of accepting the results of international interdependence has been seen in such projects as the Optional

Clause and the General Act of Arbitration under the League, and more concretely, though less universally, in the various treaties for Western co-operation since the Second World War which have culminated in the Atlantic Pact. All these have represented definite and tangible invasions of the principle of state-sovereignty, for each of them has meant that the states which have accepted them have, to that extent, become no longer free to act in their discretion. So also the theory of mandates and trusteeship for non-self-governing territories, the rights guaranteed to national minorities within certain member-states of the League, and the less definite competence of the United Nations to protect human rights generally, are a recognition that the days of state-independence have definitely passed. We cannot secure the necessary co-ordination between modern states except by subjecting them to a common superior. And the logic of that subjection is the primacy of the legal imperatives made by that superior over all wills which may seek to invade them. This indeed, is the position theoretically approximated to in the powers conferred on the Security Council by the United Nations Charter.

Confronted by this position, certain thinkers of distinction have sought to reconcile it with the older view in two ways. On the one hand they have argued that international law is merely national law since its operative force depends upon its acceptance by individual states; on the other they have insisted that while international law is effectively law, it is a system complete in itself, independent of the will of individual states, and having no connection therewith. But neither view is satisfactory. To the first two replies may be made. On the evidence, states consent to the rules of international law not because they so choose, but because they have, in fact, no alternative, and there is no gain in preserving a theory of consent which, in fact, is mostly fictional in character. While, also, no international law can possibly be operative except as its subjects consent to its imposition, that is true also of the law of the state itself. Juristically, that is to say, to make the legal character of international law dependent upon its success in getting applied is to apply to it canons of validity which the jurist does not dream of applying to national law. Upon his own postulates, legality has reference only to a source competent to make the rules involved. It is, for him, a question of competence purely; and he is compelled to reject hypotheses which import criteria built upon other considerations. Nor is the notion of international law as an autonomous system independent of national law more satisfactory. For the whole purpose of international law is to regulate the behaviour of citizens living, by definition, in states. It cannot achieve its purpose save by binding the will of states to its end. To do so, its inherent superiority to this will is inescapable; and we are driven to assume that municipal law is derived from the postulates which international law requires.

One final argument may be considered. It is simple, it is said, to view the state as a legal order because there comes at once into view a body of men entitled by their position to impose its imperatives upon its citizens; in the society of states, this clarity of imposition is lacking. If one of its rules is broken, there is no one upon whom the obligation directly rests to apply a sanction for the infraction which has occurred. But before we accept this criticism as fatal, it is important to consider its implications. It assumes that law is created by an organ of the state which has the power to apply sanctions where necessary. This, in fact, is to assume the classical theory of sovereignty as we have inherited it from Hobbes and Austin; and that theory, as we have seen, fails to fit the complicated conditions of modern society. We are less concerned with the discovery of a common superior by whose will all law is made than to find appropriate organs for making necessary rules in the different departments of social life; it is the division, and not the unification, of functions which chiefly interests us. Nor is this all. We can argue that many of the rules of international law are normally and naturally applied by the ordinary courts of justice in a state; and the famous decision of Lord Parker in the *Zamora*[1] shows how far they are prepared to go in this direction. We can argue, also, that international rules are now applied not only in the International Court of Justice, but also that its decisions shape increasingly the character of the work done in all bodies concerned with similar material.

It is obvious, moreover, that the League and the United Nations, with all their imperfections, have been an institutional expression of the idea of sanction. The tendency of their common history has been towards giving this idea stronger form. A Covenant which began by the idea of delaying the onset of war in the hope that an interval might provide that reflection out of which successful mediation emerges, moved towards the notion that aggressive action could be defined, and that the state deemed responsible for aggression must incur the enmity of all members of the League. And the chief difference of principle between the United Nations and the League lies precisely in this point: that the Security Council of the United Nations is invested with the fullest executive powers on behalf of the members of the United Nations, who are pledged in advance to support whatever decisions it may make. Under the Covenant of the League the forms of corporate responsibility were rudimentary; under the United Nations Charter they have become explicit and definite. The Council of the League already functioned, if not as a cabinet, at least as a body whose resemblance to an ordinance-making body was important; the Security Council of the United Nations is, in principle, definitely such a body, possessing supreme legal competence, however

[1] (1916) 2 A. C. 93.

much it is crippled in practice by the need for unanimity among the Great Powers. The League Assembly, furthermore, had a direct effect on public opinion that was impressive; and the General Assembly of the United Nations (though theoretically possessing less powers than the League Assembly in proportion as the Security Council possesses more powers than the League Council) has also shown a surprising vitality and tendency to extend its scope. Defective and misused as the machinery of the League and the United Nations may have been, it can at least be said of them that the peoples of the world have looked to them to limit and control the excesses of individual states. Of their work in social and scientific service, one can say with justice that had it not been performed the world would be a poorer and uglier place; and were it to cease, it would have to be invented.

The League suffered much from the absence of the United States throughout its existence, and of Russia for all save its last five years. But it was destroyed neither by this, nor by its own procedural defects, but by the subordinating of the obligations it imposed to the continued sovereignty of its members. The United Nations includes both the United States and Russia, but continues to face the fundamental contradiction between sovereign liberties, now restricted in form as well as in fact to the Great Powers, and international co-operation. The veto power must, however, probably be regarded as inevitable in a body which there is not yet the will to convert into a world government, and it is wiser to look for limitation of the veto in the growth of conventions about its employment rather than in the revision of the Charter. But, despite their weaknesses and their setbacks, it is difficult to doubt both the value of the League and the United Nations and the necessity for an organisation of this kind. It is clear that the founding of the League of Nations represented a decisive stage in the history of political institutions.

F

II

An institution like the League or the United Nations can only develop by the continuous restriction of the rights of individual states. What, in fact, is involved in its successful evolution is its expression of a power, within an increasingly wider field, to limit the subject-matter upon which states are entitled to legislate upon their own initiative. It will tend to assume authority to lay down ways of behaviour for states in all matters of common concern to international society. Some, at least, of these matters define themselves. The right to make war, the definition of frontiers, the scale of armaments, tariffs and migration, the protection of backward races, these are all subjects upon which the individual state is not likely to retain final competence over any long period. This is not the less true if, owing to the paralysis of the United Nations through disagreement between the Great Powers, the process of international integration is being concentrated first of all in the two great groups that have emerged from the Second World War, the one controlled by the Cominform, the other organised in the Atlantic Pact. For these things represent the beginning, and not the end, of the evolution which, doubtless only after long travail, we are destined to witness.

The development of science in industry in the past century has had vast effects on the international community. The power to produce has, through the unequal distribution of purchasing power, greatly outstripped the power to consume. The result has been that states with a modern technical equipment have entered into feverish competition for export markets and been driven to protect their standards of living against competition from states with a lower standard. The consequence of this condition must sooner or later be the international control of raw materials, of methods of marketing, and of standards of labour. The League of Nations was brought increasingly to realise the importance of the economic causes of war, and this recognition was given institutional form in the creation of the Economic and Social Council of the United Nations. Moreover, one of the chief causes of chaos in the inter-war years was the uncontrolled right of the individual state to determine its monetary policy. A drastic restriction of credit in Washington could cause a disastrous fall in world prices; a reckless heaping up of gold in Paris might mean unemployment in Japan and South America. Since the Second World War international organs have been developed to give more effective expression to the interdependence of modern finance. It is common sense to infer that the World Bank, the International Monetary Fund, and any European payments union administered by the Bank of International Settlements at Basle are the beginning of a central monetary system of which states will become dependent units in much the same way as the English joint-stock banks are subordinate to the Bank of England.

One may visualise, further, a development upon a different plane. So far, and, in the light of historical conditions, quite intelligibly, international law has too little concerned itself with the rights of individuals regarded as persons entitled in them-selves to its protection. If they have been foreigners who have suffered at the hands of an alien state, they have had to look to their own state for remedy; and there have been no means of compelling that state to assist them to procure justice. Where a citizen has been dealt with unjustly by his own state, that has been regarded by international law as a matter of domestic jurisdiction outside of its competence. The state, it has been argued, is a sovereign state; no one, therefore, in this realm, has the right to question decisions it may feel called upon to make.

It is not, however, impossible that we are at the beginning of a new epoch in these matters. There is no theoretic reason why, granted a suitable procedure, a foreigner injured unjustly by the action of an alien state should not be entitled to seek redress in a body like the International Court of Justice. He should, doubtless, be able not only to prove his case, but also to show that he has exhausted the remedies for his protection which the offending state itself provides. There is no reason, either, why, under suitable circumstances, the national of a given state who is denied rights to the observance of which that state is pledged by international law, should not be able to call the offending state to account for its torts in an international court. The Minorities Treaties which formed part of the peace settlement of 1919 gave the Eastern European minorities, so long as the authority of the League endured, a degree of protection under the League council, with the possibility of reference to the Permanent Court. The United Nations Declaration of Human Rights is a broader application of the same principle. Though it is of moral not legal force, it is the first step towards an International Bill of Rights, and this in turn would imply enforcement through a protocol of implementation giving individuals the right unilaterally to bring an action in an international tribunal against their own states, with effective sanctions against states for violation of the international law of human rights. The project of making the individual a subject of international law with enforceable rights against his own government is still in its infancy; but the more we can develop the understanding that the individual is the person for whose defence international law exists, the more ample will be its binding force upon men. Similarly, it is possible to see, since the Second World War, the beginnings of an effective international criminal law. The trial and punishment of war crimes committed by nationals of the Axis Powers has been more systematic than ever before. For the first time in history, at the International Military Tribunal at Nuremberg, the political leaders of a sovereign state were tried for planning and waging aggressive war defined as a crime. This was a new judicial process, but the moral judgment it enforced, that aggressive war is a crime against humanity, was at least a generation old; and the Nuremberg Trial thus represented a growth in the application of law analogous to that by which the common law itself grew up.

The implications of this are worth consideration. A hundred years ago, it was as natural for Austin to stop his discussion of law at the boundaries of the state as it would have been impossible for the medieval thinker to discuss it in other than universal terms. Austin's world was one in which the state seemed the last term in the evolution of institutions; competition was its law, and behind that competition was the idea, inherited from the benevolent optimism of the eighteenth century, that Nature in the long run rights everything if we trust only to her unfettered discretion. It is the same optimism as one sees in the 'invisible hand' of Adam Smith; in the eager affirmation of Benthamite radicalism that liberty of contract is the final cure for social ills; and in the teaching of Hegel that the lesson of historical evolution is the attainment of an even greater freedom.

Our world is a different world. What impresses us is not national separation but international dependence, not the value of competition, but the necessity for co-operation. We have learned that the state cannot live, as Aristotle thought, a self-sufficient life if it is to have peaceful and coherent contact with other states; it is a part of the great society the wants of which interpenetrate every aspect of its being. We have come to see that the conferment of liberty of contract upon the individual is meaningless without equality of bargaining power. The ideal of sovereign states, in fact, has become as dangerous as the older ideal of isolated individuals set over against the state to which they belong. We have to make a functional theory of society in which power is organised for ends which are clearly implied in the materials we are compelled to use. The notion that this power can be left to the unfettered discretion of any section of society has been revealed as incompatible with the good life. The sovereignty of the state in the world to which we belong is as obsolete as the sovereignty of the Roman Church three hundred years ago.

We cannot, that is to say, leave the hinterland between states unorganised; and as soon as we envisage its organisation, it is obvious that the sovereignty of the state means anarchy. It is entitled to control matters of local reference; it cannot be left to exploit matters in which other states are involved. In our position, therefore, the natural approach to the problems of politics is to view the state as a province of the great society, and to insist, accordingly, that its rules are limited by their necessary subordination to wider interests beyond. We may agree that it is a tremendous task to organise the great society, to discover the institutions appropriate to the field it must control. But nothing is more likely to make that effort success-ful than deliberate thought in those terms. The more con-sciously we admit that the sovereignty of the state expressed an historical condition which has now passed, the more likely we are to think in terms of a jurisprudence which fits our new environment. A new world cannot hope to live adequately by the categories of the old.

It is possible, on the other hand, that our effort at inter-national organisation may break down. Institutions which have accreted power do not easily surrender their authority. A state which was once Leviathan does not take amiably to the hook. Anyone who considers the possibilities of conflict that we confront, the racial hatreds, the national and even religious jealousies, the economic rivalries, above all the antagonism be-tween Russia and America that has emerged from the Second World War, may be pardoned for concluding that the prospects of peace are infinitely small. In the League Covenant and in the United Nations Charter we have paid lip-service to the ideal of disarmament; but we have not disarmed, and to-day we live under the threat of armaments more terrible than any the world has known before. We have eulogised the principle of trusteeship: but we have endeavoured, so far as we can, to conduct our mandates and trust territories on the old colonial theses. There is much that entitles us to be hopeful, such as the grant of independence to India which Macaulay, more than a century ago, said would be the proudest day in English history. Nevertheless, the dogmas and orthodoxies, the cruelties and the fanaticism that have accompanied the development of the Communist experiment in Russia and Eastern Europe, the racial and class conflicts that are inherent in the national awakening of Asia and of Africa, the unsolved problems of the future of Germany and Japan, the growth of political witch-hunting and hostility to unorthodox ideas in America, these forbid us to imagine that progress is an inevitable idea. There is neither freedom nor happiness save as we make them; there is neither freedom nor happiness save as we make peace. We have to learn to think of it as a creative adventure, involving sacrifices as momentous, risks as great, as were ever involved in war. We have to prove our right to it by our willingness to pay the price for which it calls.

No one can have the assurance that we shall succeed. If we know the road to the goal, we shrink from the travail of the journey; more, there are not a few, and those mostly powerful men, who announce with emphasis their rejection of the goal. To attain it, the great state must humble itself, the rich are called upon to sacrifice. We cannot be free save as we are just; and the price of justice is equality. We have no inherent reason to suppose that those who possess, and enjoy, power will surrender it for ideals they do not share. If they fight to retain their authority, they have at least a bare prospect of success. If they win, as the recent history of Germany and Italy has shown, they establish tyranny within, and the prospect of anarchy without; if they lose, as the history of Russia makes manifest, the prospects are no different. The victory of peace depends upon an intense and widespread will to peace; and that will can be neither intense nor widespread so long as the interest in its consequences is so different. The idea of sacrifice for the sake of righteousness is not yet a part of the mental habits of mankind. We have not even learned to tolerate gladly where we feel differently. Our conflicts have still all the bitterness of creed-wars; only the substance of the creeds has changed.

A generation, in fact, like our own, whose feet lie so near to the abyss, has no right to optimism about its future; the fact that it knows the way is no proof that it will choose the way. In this, paradoxically enough, there lies perhaps our greatest hope. The dangers about us are so tangible and immediate that we are driven to experiment and innovation. We have learned by tragic experience the fragility of civilised habits; we may also have learned the danger of seeking again to test their strength. The mere knowledge that further conflict on any widespread scale will make the inheritance of civilisation something less than a memory may stir us to the temper in which justice is no longer an empty ideal. There could be, after all, a common interest in the good life; and the very difficulty of its attainment might lead to the realisation of its beauty.

A NOTE ON BOOKS

Much the best way to study politics is by reading critically its classical texts. Any full list of these would occupy more space than is possible here. But the reader should at least be aware of the following:

Plato, *The Republic*, translated with introduction and notes by F. M. Cornford (Clarendon Press, 1946).

Aristotle, *The Politics*, translated with an introduction, notes and appendices by Ernest Barker (Oxford University Press, 1946).

St. Augustine, *The City of God*, translated by Marcus Dods (Edinburgh, Clark, 2 vols., 1913).

Dante, *De Monarchia*, translated by P. H. Wicksteed, in *A Translation of the Latin Works of Dante Alighieri* (Dent, Temple Classics, 1904).

Thomas Hobbes, *Leviathan*, edited with an introduction by Michael Oakeshott (Blackwell, 1946).

John Locke, *The Second Treatise of Civil Government*, edited with an introduction by J. W. Gough (Blackwell, 1946).

Jean-Jacques Rousseau, *Du Contrat Social*, edited by C. E. Vaughan (Manchester University Press, 1918); *The Social Contract*, translated by G. D. H. Cole (Dent, Everyman's Library, 1913).

Edmund Burke, *Reflections on the Revolution in France*, in *The Works of Edmund Burke*, Vol. IV (Oxford University Press, World's Classics, 1907).

John Stuart Mill, *On Liberty, and Considerations on Representative Government*, edited with an introduction by R. B. McCallum (Blackwell, 1946).

T. H. Green, *Lectures on the Principles of Political Obligation* (Longmans, 1895).

Karl Marx and Friedrich Engels *The Communist Manifesto*, available in *The Essential Left* (Unwin Books, 1960).

The more modern debate may be studied in the following:

G. D. H. Cole, *Social Theory* (Methuen, 1920).

R. M. MacIver, *The Modern State* (Oxford University Press, 1926).

H. J. Laski, *Liberty in the Modern State* (Faber, 1930).

Lord Hugh Cecil, *Conservatism* (Thornton Butterworth, Home University Library, 1912).

W. Y. Elliott, *The Pragmatic Revolt in Politics* (New York, Macmillan, 1928).

Léon Duguit, *Law in the Modern State*, translated by Frida and Harold Laski (Allen & Unwin, 1921).

L. T. Hobhouse, *The Metaphysical Theory of the State* (Allen & Unwin, 1918).

Hans Kelsen, *Allgemeine Staatslehre* (Berlin, Springer, 1925); *General Theory of Law and State*, translated by Anders Wedberg (Harvard University Press, 1945).

R. Carré de Malbert, *Contribution à la Théorie Générale de l'Etat* (Paris, Sirey, 2 vols, 1920-2).

R. H. Tawney, *The Acquisitive Society* (Bell, 1921); *Equality* (Allen & Unwin, 1931).

J. P. Plamenatz, *Consent, Freedom and Political Obligation* (Oxford University Press, 1938).

Michael Oakeshott, *The Social and Political Doctrines of Contemporary Europe* (Cambridge University Press, 1939).

Ignazio Silone, *The School for Dictators*, translated by Gwenda David and Eric Mosbacher (Cape, 1939).

E. F. M. Durbin, *The Politics of Democratic Socialism* (Routledge, 1940).

R. G. Collingwood, *The New Leviathan* (Clarendon Press, 1942).

Sir Ernest Barker, *Reflections on Government* (Oxford University Press, 1942).

T. D. Weldon, *States and Morals* (Murray, 1946).

J. D. Mabbott, *The State and the Citizen* (Hutchinson's University Library, 1948).

GEORGE ALLEN & UNWIN LTD

London: 40 Museum Street, W.C.1

Auckland: P.O. Box 36013, Northcote Central, N.4
Barbados: P.O. Box 222, Bridgetown
Beirut: Deeb Building, Jeanne d'Arc Street
Bombay: 15 Graham Road, Ballard Estate, Bombay 1
Buenos Aires: Escritorio 454-459, Florida 165
Calcutta: 17 Chittaranjan Avenue, Calcutta 13
Cape Town: 68 Shortmarket Street
Hong Kong: 105 Wing On Mansion, 26 Hancow Road, Kowloon
Ibadan: P.O. Box 62
Karachi: Karachi Chambers, McLeod Road
Madras: Mohan Mansions, 38c Mount Road, Madras 6
Mexico: Villalongin, 32 Mexico 5, D.F.
Nairobi: P.O. Box 30583
New Delhi: 13-14 Asaf Ali Road, New Delhi 1
Ontario: 81 Curlew Drive, Don Mills
Philippines: Manila, P.O. Box 4322
Rio de Janeiro: Caixa Postal 2537-Zc-00
Singapore: 36c Prinsep Street, Singapore 7
Sydney, N.S.W.: Bradbury House, 55 York Street
Tokyo: P.O. Box 26, Kamata

HAROLD LASKI

THE STATE IN THEORY AND PRACTICE

'Penetrating, courageous, and incisive account of the modern State merits the closest attention of all political thinkers in this country. . . . Professor Laski's closely reasoned statement should form the basis of discussion in every circle of serious political thinkers.'—*The Guardian*.

'The bravest and probably the most fundamental argument for Socialism that has yet appeared in our language. . . . A book so unusual and unflinching as this from a man in his position is much more than a book: it is an event. It marks a phase in the breakdown of the capitalist system.'— H. N. Brailsford in the *Daily Herald*.

'Professor Laski is most interesting when he is most provocative, and there is much in his latest book on the functions and powers of the State to stimulate thought and arouse controversy. . . . The first couple of hundred pages are devoted to a brilliant survey of the philosophic ideas regarding the duties of the State.'—*Sunday Times*.

'An important contribution to current politics. . . . Mr. Laski becomes brilliant in his second long chapter. It is an analysis of the State as it is to-day.'—*New Statesman and Nation*.

REFLECTIONS ON THE REVOLUTION OF OUR TIME

This is the first paperback edition of this great classic. In her Foreword to this edition Mrs Laski writes: 'On a recent visit to India I was overwhelmed by the number of my husband's ex-students who came to shake my hand and to tell me how much this book had meant to them – to succeeding generations of students in India and elsewhere over forty years. That is why I have acceded to the Publishers' request that I add a few words to this new edition.

'This book was written by my husband in 1924, before he became involved in Party politics. But already then he stressed the inevitable disasters to the world if we did not concern ourselves with the need to change; that government by tradition must be replaced by government by consent.

'During the last decade there have been revolutionary changes throughout the world. This revolution is still going on. Imperialism has been destroyed, in a great many places with difficulty. Colonialism has gone, but the nuclear age has arrived. There is an even greater need for inspired leadership and dynamism in the developing countries, where education has hitherto been denied. The modern world has now the knowledge, that it did not possess until the end of the Second World War, that it can conquer poverty. It remains to be seen if we have the desire to apply ourselves to this end. . . .

'My husband once said that every time an intellectual has the chance to speak out against injustices, and yet remains silent, he contributes to the moral paralysis and intellectual barrenness that grips the affluent world. It is my hope that this book will inspire many of today's students to understand the obligations of World Citizenship in an age that is becoming more difficult to understand and therefore more in need of serious thought.'

THE RISE OF EUROPEAN LIBERALISM

'As an introduction to the subject it cannot but be of the greatest utility to students.'—Bertrand Russell in *New Statesman*.

HAROLD LASKI

A GRAMMAR OF POLITICS

'A remarkable book. . . . It is impossible in this brief sketch to convey an adequate impression of this brilliant book. . . . Such a book, surveying things as they are in the light of what they must become, was needed.'—Lord Haldane in *The Observer*.

The work is not only a full discussion of the basis of political institutions, but also a series of concrete and practical proposals for the reconstruction of the social order.

'Of great importance . . . among the ablest contributions to political science in our time.'—*Hibbert Journal*.

LIBERTY IN THE MODERN STATE

The enquiry is conducted with the depth of analytical penetration, the wide reference to history and the persuasive suggestion of remedy that were characteristic of Professor Laski. This new edition is, quoting the author, 'more fully adapted to the experience through which we have passed'.

PARLIAMENTARY GOVERNMENT IN ENGLAND

'. . . the book is indispensable to any student of politics. . . . The claim that it is a true successor to Bagehot's *English Constitution* is . . . justified.'—*A.M.A.*

'His book has an excitement which derives from the dynamic quality of its subject-matter . . . difficult to put it down.'—*The Friend*.

GEORGE ALLEN & UNWIN LTD